Help
Your Child
For Life

MAUREEN MILLER

ARGUS COMMUNICATIONS A Division of **DLM** Inc.
Niles, Illinois 60648

Cover design: Gene Tarpey

Cover photo: Brent Jones

Photo credits:

Richard L. Capps 101, 186, 220

Earl L. Kubis 22

Jean-Claude Le Jeune 12, 20, 24, 32, 35, 37, 41, 42, 55, 59, 66, 83, 98, 108, 111, 117, 121, 126, 129, 132, 141, 160, 175, 179, 181, 182, 183, 184, 189, 194, 206

Acknowledgements

Grateful acknowledgement is made to the authors and publishers for permission to reprint the following: From *The People, Yes* by Carl Sandburg, copyright 1936 by Harcourt Brace Jovanovich, Inc.; renewed 1964 by Carl Sandburg. Reprinted by permission of the publishers.

Excerpt from p. 9 in *On Caring* by Milton Mayeroff, Volume Forty-three of *World Perspectives Series,* planned and edited by Ruth Nanda Anshen. Copyright © 1971 by Milton Mayeroff. By permission of Harper & Row, Publishers, Inc.

From *Complete Poems 1913-1962* by E. E. Cummings, copyright 1938 by E. E. Cummings; copyright © 1963, 1966 by Marion Morehouse Cummings. Reprinted by permission of Harcourt Brace Jovanovich, Inc. Also with the permission of MacGibbon & Kee Ltd/Granada Publishing LTD.

Adapted from "The Feel Wheel" by Anthony L. Rose, Martin J. Thommes, and Layne A. Longfellow. Reprinted with permission from *Psychology Today Magazine.* Copyright © 1972 Ziff-Davis Publishing Company.

From the *Collected Poems of William Butler Yeats.* Copyright 1906 by Macmillan Publishing Co., Inc., renewed 1934 by William Butler Yeats. Reprinted with permission of Macmillan Publishing Co., Inc. Also reprinted with permission of Miss Anne Yeats and Senator Michael Yeats.

ARGUS COMMUNICATIONS
7440 Natchez Avenue
Niles, Illinois 60648

International Standard Book Number 0-89505-018-8
Library of Congress Number 78-63105

0 9 8 7 6 5 4 3 2 1

This book is dedicated

To my parents,
who let me explore an opening-up world
and find that, though it was beautiful,
it could also hurt,
but that I could still feel comfortable in it;
who "were there" when I found the world
painful as well as beautiful;
who helped me be free—
to keep discovering myself.

I love you for what you are
knowing so well what you are.
And I love you more yet, child,
deeper yet than ever, child,
for what you are going to be.

Carl Sandburg

Contents

Preface 7

section 1 Introduction 13

section 2 Helping Your Child Feel
Worthwhile 33

section 3 Creativity 97

section 4 Language, Learning,
and Living 161

Bibliography
References 227

This is a "begin-at-the-beginning" book for parents and all who care for children during those vitally formative years from birth to six. It is designed not just to be read but also to be used as a journal-workbook for you as you participate in your children's journey into life. It focuses on your role in developing their self-esteem, creativity, and language and learning abilities, for your influence in these three areas can radiate through all of their life. It can help them develop competency and inner resources; it can help them cope more effectively with a rapidly moving world.

Helping your children go forth to their engagement with life can be one of the most creative adventures you have ever undertaken.

This book is written from a mosaic of perspectives—I have conducted numerous workshops for parents and teachers over the past four years; I have learned from, and listened to, many parents, watched and learned from their children, taught both adolescents and adults, worked with delinquent girls and with men and women who late in life came to feel some sort of personal worth, and, of course, I have for years been a parent myself.

As I shared with others, they shared with me. When I was a teacher, those I taught became my teacher. They helped reaffirm in me that it all begins in the home—at the beginning.

HOW THE BOOK IS STRUCTURED

This book is divided into three main sections, each building upon the other. Each section is treated separately only so that each can be more clearly grasped. In reality, they are interdependent. They work together to develop your children's competency, inner strengths, and ability to cope in today's world.

I. HELPING YOUR CHILD FEEL WORTHWHILE focuses on your child's self-esteem, its necessity for successful living, and your major role in developing this positive self-image. It offers patterns of communication and a variety of activities to share with your child to strengthen self-esteem and affect every area of his or her life.

II. CREATIVITY AND LEARNING demonstrates the link between the creative process and learning and shows ways you can nourish creativity and learning to develop your child's inner resources: independence, hope, freedom to fail, ability to solve problems, and the ability to deal effectively with change.

III. LANGUAGE, LEARNING, AND LIVING traces the development of a child's language and learning; emphasizes your part in developing these abilities; offers specific ways to foster language, learning, and intellectual skills; and shows how this can be accomplished in daily living.

8

A variety of self-inventories and personal exercises are included throughout the book to help you more fully understand yourself and record your progress in developing your child's self-esteem, creativity and language ability. These are designed so they can be used singly by parents or anyone caring for a child. They can be used by parents together to share individual perceptions and deepen a real communication, and they can be used by groups so that members can benefit from sharing individual experiences and reactions and can feel strengthened by a common goal. In all cases, working through these inventories and exercises offers valuable self-evaluation and a charting of your activities and insights according to the child's needs.

Some of the suggestions in this book are extensions of material shared by concerned dads, moms, parents, and grandparents in *The Family Learning Center For Growth and Getting Along Together Workshops* I have conducted over the past years. They are extensions of lively interchanges in which parents said such things as, "I always thought I was the only one with problems. I never knew other people had the same problems," and "I wish I had known some of these things twenty years ago." As you join in the use of these materials, may you also feel that you are joining in that wider human family: of all who are concerned with helping a child—for life.

In so doing, I hope you can reach these goals: To learn and put into practice ways of helping your children develop the inner resources needed for coping with life; to know that these resources can be strengthened by helping your children feel good about themselves; to stimulate their creative expression and develop their use of language; and to realize that each of these goals works with the other to help each child be the person he or she can be.

section
1

Introduction

To care for someone, I must know
many things. I must know, for example,
who the other is, what his powers
and limitations are, what his needs are,
and what is conducive to his growth:
I must know how to respond to his needs,
and what my own powers and limitations are.

Milton Mayeroff

Children's Needs:
Their Pattern of Growth

From infancy on, your children are reaching toward independence and the ability to take charge of themselves. You can see this in the background of children's early growth stages and can begin to measure their needs—and the way they should be answered.

Essential to every child's development, indeed to every human's development are:

- Achievements to help show them they are capable.
- Responsibilities to add to their sense of accomplishment.
- Security of the familiar and comfort of a routine.
- Acceptance of themselves and of their attempts at new things.
- Affection, with signs to help show that they are valued and secure, signs of love despite their increased independence.
- Balance between being too harsh and too easy. If you are too harsh, your children might want to "get even." If you are too lenient, they might inwardly doubt your love.
- Respect and understanding of their individuality.

These factors are important in infancy and throughout life, but the forms they take, the ways they are furthered will differ at different stages of your child's life.

This development can be marked according to three separate periods to trace in general how children grow. In no way is this meant to offer rigid guidelines for individual children. Every home is different. Part of your challenge as parents is to meet the paradox of letting each child be an individual while also "fitting in."

FROM INFANCY
TO EIGHTEEN MONTHS

Children discover themselves and their world through the adults who care for them. Through their earliest experiences, they learn whether the world is kind or cruel, trustworthy or untrustworthy. And, though life will show them that goodness is not always present, they need a base of trust in their environment and its people to feel comfortable. How well they will feel this trust, how well they will fit their particular talents into life, how well they will cope and contribute, to what degree will they reach their potential—the answer to these questions begins with you. You are the ones they first know. The impression you make will be lifelong.

This is stamped inside them as you respond to their needs for food, shelter, security, and to that very important need to feel loveable and worthwhile. Attention to physical needs allows time for attention to emotional needs. It all can be accomplished in day-by-day living. Through the warmth of their mothers' bodies as they are being fed, the comfort in their parents' arms as they are being held and tended to, the tones in the parents' voices, infants begin to absorb the feeling that they are valued. They feel good.

Not only your warmth and security *but also the emotional overtones of how you feel about yourselves will seep into them to start forming their opinion of themselves.* From that base, they begin to know whether they stand on shaky or firm ground in their newly discovered world.

They have just weathered the crisis of birth. They have just begun to exist as separate creatures suddenly thrust into a world full of discomforts. They soon learn that these discomforts can be relieved through your responses. They are beginning to know love.

Their image of themselves is gradually taking shape. They come to realize that one of their hands can hold the other and that "this part of me is different from the blanket I hold in my hands." Their first gurgling gives way to louder expressions, and they begin to keep time to simple rhythms. The infants' world is becoming more stable, and they feel increasingly at home in it.

They begin to sit up, crawl, and move around. Experiences are multiplying in their world and, for a time, they themselves feel at the center of this universe. As they continue to move about, they feel better about themselves and more independent. They realize they are beginning to have some control of their surroundings. They find an ever-widening area around them and know they can reach it of their own power. Inner resources of independence and self-worth are being formed.

Their separateness from those who nourish them expands as they grow. They pull themselves up, walk around objects by hanging on to them, and realize a growing coordination of arms and legs and body. They feel more to-gether as they are putting themselves to-gether. Increasingly, they feel responsible for taking charge of themselves.

These early months are times of intense learning. Curiosity keeps pushing them to move and learn more and want to do things themselves. All of this learning and achieve-ment gives satisfaction. They are additions to the "I-am-worthwhile" picture they are form-ing of themselves.

They begin to try out some syllables they have heard, and the sounds bring a response from the special persons with whom they feel so close. The pictures they have had in their mind are now tied in with symbols they them-selves have spoken. Syllables become their first word. With language, another mastery over their environment has begun.

Their early clinging to supports gives way to trying a few steps by themselves. They learn to walk. Now they have additional confidence—both from having mastered the once unman-ageable and from their family's delight in their accomplishment.

New words are added; the things they walk around and touch and eat are given names. Language helps them name the objects that were only pictures in their minds, and curiosity keeps them moving on to new discoveries and new pictures.

This curiosity is an essential ingredient of learning, creativity, and motivation. Take care not to stifle it. Allow them enough freedom to move about. Give them the security of limits, for even at this age when exploration is so necessary to learning, limits are vital. Too wide a world can be frightening.

Exploration can bring alluring dangers. Children learn through the senses. They taste, touch, and swallow in order to learn. They make no distinction between poisons, powders, and polishes under the sink, the scrap of cookie on the floor, or the animal cracker on their high chair.

From birth through the toddling years, they have learned much. They have grown physically and have increased their inner stature. From complete dependence on you, they have reached out and away by mastering walking, talking, handling eating utensils and innumerable objects—and handling their bodies in space. They have learned the names of those close to them and that they fit into the picture. They feel love for you who answered their needs, anger if their needs are not met, and fear that you might disappear.

Depending on how you have responded to them and the inner stirrings they have felt about your caring for them—and yourself— they have learned to trust. They are able to feel, "I can depend on them. I like it here."

FROM EIGHTEEN MONTHS
TO THREE YEARS

Through play, talk, physical affection, the freedom to explore and to be curious, and through limits, you continue to meet your children's needs as they are moving into an ever wider world. They are developing a new completeness. Their push to grow continues the push to find out about themselves and their world. They need to feel the satisfaction that comes from accomplishment and exploration. They also, of course, continue to need your love. And telling them no as you guide them is part of that love. It helps them learn what they can and cannot do.

In telling them no, you are taking a first step in the formation of their conscience. Hearing you say no is part of that negative phase in which they soon say no in imitation of you. With the individuality they feel and the power they realize in the word, they also feel that somehow they have to test themselves against you—the person who has power over them. This is not disrespect, but a sign of growing to be a person. They are developing an increased awareness of themselves as they interact with their family. For them no is part of learning to know more of who they are and where they fit into the world.

The smallest details are important to this learning. Children learn by minute observation and exploration through the senses—by tasting and handling the ice and letting it melt away in the mouth or fingers or glass, by chewing the pieces of paper—or the soap. They pull petals from flowers, not to be bad, but to find out—the petals are soft, and they come out easily between little fingers. They dip a washcloth in the toilet bowl, not to be bad, but because the water is enticing, and they have control over it. It gives them a sense of power to look at the water and to move their hands around in it. They want to try things out themselves. *You* have to judge when to say no.

Children's first stumbling steps give way to confidence and the desire to try new things.

Success helps them feel good about themselves, and this leads them to find new successes. So, let them have a chance for success. And let them know that when they fall down, they can try again.

Life can be very confusing for children. You smile fondly when they scribble on paper, but when they scrawl over the invitingly white wall at the side of the bed, you don't smile at all; you take the pencil away. Your repeated no's reinforce in their minds that this is something that must not be done, and that they will please you by not doing it. Gradually they learn inner control and that they can feel good about

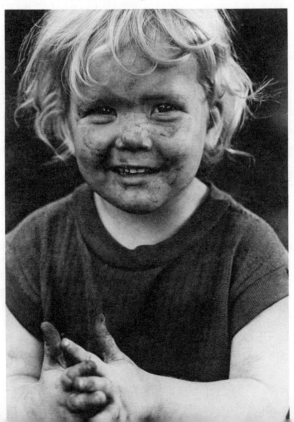

calling a halt on themselves. The controls for wanting to please grow in them, and they gain additional strength from not doing. They are developing inner resources for control, which can serve as a pattern for self-control in later years and help form a conscience.

From two to three, there is a great burst of language, and continued experiences add to children's use of it. Likewise, they feel the mastery that accompanies language. It, too, helps them feel good about themselves.

These feelings mix with others, pleasant and unpleasant. You can provide a healthy outlet for their feelings by providing for physical activities such as riding a rocking horse, climbing steps, swinging on a swing, swishing water in the kitchen sink.

New accomplishments delight them, and they delight you. Let your children catch your approval. They are pleased with themselves when you are pleased with them. Avoid pushing them too hard. Avoid having them think they are valued only for their accomplishments. They are learning so much, and too many demands on them can cause them to be unsure of themselves.

They are learning more about the world and are learning more about themselves and their bodies. Their bodies are important to them. Exploration of all parts of themselves is as natural as it was with anything else about which they were learning.

During this two-to-three-year stage, their intellectual vistas have broadened considerably. They are growing up, but they still need to feel physical love. Hugs and cuddling give them security and tell them they are valued.

Opposite forces keep working within them. They need security, but they are more and more independent. "Don't hold my hand," and "Let me do it myself," are part of this independence, and their own reaching to later responsibility. Allow them that independence. It helps show them that they are capable.

Imagination allows for make-believe play, for developing imaginary friends, for developing fantasy and fears. Their fears are very real—fears of going down the toilet, of loud noises, of being left alone, of any number of things. Avoid shaming, or making fun of their fears. They are part of them, and making fun of part of them can weaken their confidence and curtail communication.

Talk to them in the darkness if they are afraid of the dark. Tell them you are there, that they are there. In the daylight, talk to them about the dark, so it becomes part of the reality of the day. Give them finger paints or marking pens and ask them to show you what the dark is like. You are accepting the reality of their fear, and you are also accepting them.

How your children feel about themselves is reflected in their behavior and in everything they do. So try to understand what they are thinking and feeling. Talk and listen to them and let them know they are accepted. This is the base for communication—understanding their needs and keeping their perspective in mind. Their world is large. It can be scary. It can be delightful. And, it cannot be swallowed whole or learned about too quickly. So think of their world and the fact that they are responding to it from a different level than you.

As they continue their rapid exploration, remember they need protection from some of the areas into which their searching curiosity can take them. But do not overprotect for that can stifle them. They must be watched but not bound in. A careful balance must be struck. The motto, "Caution, children at play," can also be interpreted as, "Caution, do not stand guard too much."

FROM THREE TO SIX

The controls and limits, freedom, security, and protection you have given your children have helped give them a base of trust, a feeling of self-esteem, and a sense of their own identity and ability. By now, you have helped in much of their basic formation.

Three-year-olds talk a lot to you, and you talk to them. They understand much of the language they will use in ordinary conversation throughout their life. They have learned to adapt to others through interaction with their family and by playing with other children. More and more, they will keep moving into a wider circle of places and people.

They are beginning to move away from their position as the center of the universe, and their first love of themselves has spread to the love of others. They are aware of themselves in relation to others, that they belong in a family, that they have friends down the street, that they have grandparents to visit. They look at family pictures and talk about them, and they look ahead to visits with cousins, aunts, and uncles. They know what happiness and sadness are and can tell you that they are happy or sad with themselves. They are also quick to spot sadness and happiness in others and can absorb the family atmosphere in times of crises. They know how others feel and can identify with them.

Climbing, sliding, running, jumping, swinging, they are much more at home with their

24

bodies and can manage them with ease. In the different pace of their days, their curiosity continues but takes different form, and, with repeated "Why's," they attempt to find answers. It is part of their new sense of determination.

As these years move on, continue to try to strike a balance between freedom and limits. Five-year-olds still need the security they always needed; and now, they find consistency in your actions and routine (of bedtime, meals, and order of events) comfortable.

As children approach kindergarten age, rules are something to be relied upon and help keep things in order. Likewise the authority of other adults, of teachers, parents, and grandparents is acceptable, for this also helps keep rules in force and things in their ordered place. And children do like home to be an ordered place. They like home. Home is good. It is comfortable. It is where they can be accepted.

To expect perfection at this age is unrealistic and can hurt your children. If they think you expect perfection and that they are only valued if perfect, they can begin to expect perfection in themselves. Knowing that they cannot really be as perfect as you (and perhaps they) want them to be can cause them to be insecure or to pretend to be better than they are. It can cause them to be unreal to themselves and to others— even at this early age.

As they go on into life this is a good time to tell yourself, "Don't expect your child to stay on a pedestal. It is such a small place to walk around on, and it is such a long way to the bottom."

Understanding Yourself and Your Child
The Beginnings of Your Journal

Taking this opening inventory can help you better understand yourself and your child. In this, and in each of the exercises throughout the book, you will be asked to look into your life and that of your child carefully and respond as the exercise applies to you or to your family. Being as honest as you can be, taking the time to really think about your responses, and then committing them to writing can help clarify your perceptions of yourself. You can see where you really are, how you want to act, or how you may want to change your actions.

name _____

1. List eight words or phrases you think best describe yourself as a parent. __

_____

_____

_____

   (Your list could include, but does not have to, words such as the following: courageous, confident, curious, independent, resourceful, patient, impatient, resilient, determined, competent, understanding, tired, free, not afraid of failure, strong, successful, self-acceptant, dignified, loveable, playful, fearful, guilty, harsh, rigid, strict.)

2. Look over your list and rank the descriptions in their order of importance in your life. Rate the characteristics which have

the most importance—1; rate the least important—8.

3. Look again at the list. What strengths have you indicated? What weaknesses? List these, or any others you think of, below. Then rank order them according to their importance in your life.

Strengths _____

_____

_____

Weaknesses _____

_____

_____

4. What do you enjoy the most about your role as a parent? _____

_____

5. What do you like the least about being a parent? _____

_____

6. What are your main concerns in being a parent? _____

_____

7. List six things you value in your life. These can be qualities such as honesty or cheerfulness; or these can be people, possessions, roles, or occupations. At one sharing session, one parent listed

"Myself," as something specially valued. Try to be as honest and self-examining as you can. _____

_____

_____

_____

_____

8. Now, list your strengths and weaknesses, and the effect each of them could have on your child.

STRENGTHS

Strengths   **Effect**

_____

_____

_____

_____

WEAKNESSES

Weaknesses   **Effect**

_____

_____

_____

_____

9. By now, you have read the preceding section summarizing the growth stages of the one- to six-year-old child. Without

referring to those pages, what needs stand out in your mind? _____

_____

_____

10. List any of these that are needs of your child. _____

_____

_____

11. Are there any needs your child has which you think you cannot meet? ___

_____

_____

_____

12. Which of the strengths you listed will help you meet your child's needs? List your child's needs in the spaces provided below. Opposite each need, write the strength that will help your child.

Your Child's Needs   **Your Strengths**

1. _____

2. _____

3. _____

4. _____

5. _____

6. _____

13. Are there any strengths which you need to develop, or which you do not have, to answer you child's needs? _____

_____

_____

14. What weaknesses did you list which will hamper your filling your child's needs?

_____

_____

15. What is the main thing you want for your child now? _____

_____

16. What is the main thing you want for your child in the future? _____

_____

_____

Go back over your inventory. Are you now more aware of your strengths? Of your child's needs? Of how your strengths can help your child? Keep your strengths in mind. Write them on a card and keep them in your billfold, or personal, prominent spot, such as on your mirror or in a desk drawer which you use often, if you need a reminder. When things begin to get you down, focus on the strengths you listed.

Think about your weaknesses. Are they really as bad as you imagine? Which has the more influence on your child's life—your strengths or your weaknesses? Concentrate on your strengths, but if you try to eliminate weaknesses, do it one day at a time, one weakness at a time. After a week, see if you made any progress in weakening the weakness. Don't expect perfection. Don't tackle the entire problem at once. Don't get discouraged. And don't focus so much on yourself that you take away from your focus on your child. Such a focus can keep you from feeling free and being natural with your child.

section 2

Helping Your Child Feel Worthwhile

who are you, little i

(five or six years old)
peering from some high

window; at the gold

of november sunset

(and feeling: that if day
has to become night

this is a beautiful way)
e. e. cummings

People respond quickly and begin to achieve as soon as they feel a sense of worth. With some, it comes so late: . . . "I never felt loved as a child, and I don't feel I am loveable now . . . . Thank you for helping me realize I am somebody . . . . I never before felt free."

But it does not have to be that way. So much can be done—at the beginning—to help a child feel he or she is somebody, that he or she is a worthwhile person, able to say, "I'm glad I'm me." It is part of the happiness that is one of our basic wants for each of our children.

HAPPINESS FOR YOUR CHILD

This is a good time to look into yourself as you answer the questions: "What makes up happiness in children? What can I do to see that my child is happy?"

Basically, happiness in childhood comes from self-acceptance, a feeling that "I am worthwhile. I do count. I am happy with being myself." This feeling of self-acceptance (or self-esteem, positive self-image, or positive self-concept) is so important that it permeates your child's whole life both now and in the future.

The picture children have of themselves is a key to their happiness. How they feel about themselves will continually reach into every area of their lives—how well they learn at home, how well they will learn in school, how they get along with their friends, and how well they are motivated to try new tasks. Their self-image affects everything they are and everything they can become. It affects their personality, their abillity to produce, to think, to create, to cope with disappointments, and to meet failure. Helping children feel worthwhile is one of the most important gifts you can give them.

This section: 1) deals with the conditions contributing to a child's feeling worthwhile; 2) focuses on self-image and on the results of positive and negative self-image; 3) outlines steps to building self-esteem, steps based on respect and understanding; 4) shows how communication can affect self-esteem; and 5) suggests activities you can share with your children to help build self-esteem.

Let us review, briefly, your children's growth patterns and how their earliest years begin to

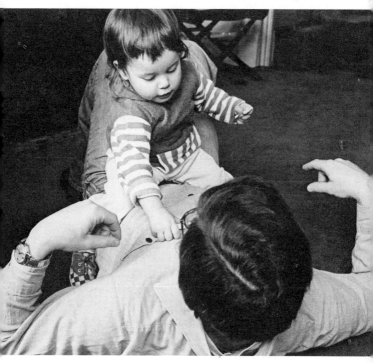

form their picture of themselves. Children's individuality is part of their human heritage. Respect this individuality. Handle it with care, for you do not want to diminish the happiness that the feeling of being unique can bring to each child. Neither do you want to lessen the unique contribution that each child can bring to the world. And yet, forces common to all children mark each individual's growth. "Every child" has common needs.

As we noted earlier, all children are pulled by diverse forces. From their youngest years they have the need for independence, a need to take charge of their lives. They also have the seemingly opposite need to find security in others. These needs do not disappear with growth. They are strong forces that continue to weave the fabric of the human condition.

What can you give your children to enable them to keep these forces in balance? Helping them feel worthwhile is one of the most positive things you can do. They need that feeling of worth to be independent, to be responsible for themselves. And they need it to free them to reach out to others, to feel that they are not losing a part of themselves, but gaining growth, in being dependent on others. (Later on, they will realize how they themselves contribute to the human family to which they are reaching. For now, you are laying the groundwork of balance.) The way you respond now in answering their needs gives them their picture of themselves. Your responses are reflected in the absorbing "inner-mirror" of the individual child.

Children begin to accept themselves through achievements, and one of their very first

achievements is that of attaining their parents' love. From this first success at feeling love, through the pulling-away stages that come with maturing, they have to test themselves against this love.

As children grow, they want to exert control over their environment. In allowing your children this freedom to move ahead, you allow them to realize successes and the satisfaction that comes from them. Crawling, walking, talking, getting along with others are achievements that help them feel good about themselves as they move on to a school-age world where outside-of-the-family influences keep adding to their picture of themselves. As you allow them the freedom (and limits) to move ahead, you allow them the freedom to fail. This can help them feel secure enough within themselves to try again.

All along the way, inner resources are being built on the awareness that they are accepted and worthwhile, that they are valued. These inner resources, which are formed early, are the basis of a continuing feeling of worth—even in the face of contradictory messages that may come along the way.

Self-acceptance and feeling worthwhile combine to make a child happy. It is as simple as that. And this comes from acceptance and affection from people important to them, from achievements, and from positive adjustments to failure.

To see how these qualities affect your child's life, look at the following diagrams. First, look at diagram A, and check those qualities which your child (or children) *evidence* or *show,* qualities contributing to their happiness. Then, in the blank boxes in diagram B, fill in qualities which would contribute to a child's unhappiness. After listing these qualities in B, place a check mark on those which your child (or children) might show.

A. The Happy Child

child's name

Feeling Worthwhile Self-Acceptance	☐	☐	☐
Acceptance	☐	☐	☐
Achievements	☐	☐	☐
Affection	☐	☐	☐
Positive Adjustment to Failure	☐	☐	☐

B. The Unhappy Child

child's name

	☐	☐	☐
	☐	☐	☐
	☐	☐	☐
	☐	☐	☐
	☐	☐	☐

39

Did you find this activity difficult—not really being sure how your child feels? This is quite normal, for how a child feels is not always readily visible. In this exercise, you were asked only to list qualities which your child *evidences,* not which you *know* he or she possesses. Such an examination as this, however, can help you to find more complete answers.

What qualities contributing to unhappiness did you list? You might have included some that stem from feelings like the following:

- I can't try again—I failed once.
- Nobody loves me.
- I can't do anything right
- I'm only valued if I'm good.
- I don't count—I'm not worth anything.

Again, you cannot know exactly how your child feels in each of these cases. You can watch to see if your child acts as if these feelings are present—this is one way of knowing your child.

Each of the conditions contributing to a child's sense of worth, to his or her self-esteem, work upon the others and enlarge them. A child cannot feel truly accepted without feeling affection. And, this is important, affection does not mean giving in to a child or putting the child on a pedestal. Real affection includes accepting a child and assisting him or her in fulfilling inner needs, needs that include freedom, control, guidance, valuing, independence, discipline, security, and limits. Acceptance of your child means accepting him or her as an individual *with these needs* common to all children. Giving your child the opportunity to fulfill needs allows him or her to experience achievements. And, as we have seen, achievements (and affection and acceptance) add to a child's feeling of self-esteem. How children feel about themselves and how much each of them is accepted for his or her individual self combine to help a child say, "I am a worthwhile person."

Perhaps you are asking, "Doesn't self-acceptance mean that one is complacent, not wanting to move ahead?"

In answer, it must be stressed that self-acceptance is a realistic sense of one's capabilities, of one's adequacies and of one's inadequacies. It is a feeling of being worthwhile enough *so that one is not afraid to continue to*

reach out to try new things, to realize more achievements, to continue to grow and to learn. Self-acceptance means being happy with oneself at a particular stage of growth and knowing that one can continue to do more and be more. It means, as a young student so simply stated, "I am somebody . . . even if all of us have faults."

You, as parents, want your children to be happy now. But, looking beyond the present, you would probably agree with the young mother who said of her child, "I want him to know there is magic in life, not just in childhood." And, in thinking of the years ahead, you want adult happiness for your children based on their ability to reach their potential. You want them to be real persons, who know their own values, with freedom to make their own choices according to those values and to assume responsibility for the choices they have made. You want them to know what they can or cannot contribute to society. To be able to do this, they must have a knowledge of who they are and a sense of personal worth. You want them to find meaning in their lives. And it all starts in childhood.

In thinking of the groundwork you are laying for your child's adult years, look carefully at the underlying influences to your children's happiness and self-esteem:

My child knows acceptance (or nonacceptance) from whom? _____

_____

And how is it shown? _____

_____

My child knows affection (or lack of affection) from whom? _____

_____

And how is it shown? _____

_____

What achievements (from what activities or what abilities) does my child realize? ____

_____

_____

What nonachievements does he or she reflect? _____

_____

What can you yourself do about your answers to the above questions? If it is a member of your family, for instance who does not show your child affection, or who spoils your child by giving in constantly, or who puts your child on a pedestal, or who values him or her only according to the child's "goodness," what can you do about it? Can your strengths influence this person? If you can't influence by your words, what part will your own attitude and example play in setting a pattern for others in the family? Remember, your child's inner-picture is being influenced by responses of others. You are one of the most important others in his or her life at this time, and how you respond to these needs is vital for your child to be able to say, "I do count."

YOUR CHILD'S INNER-PICTURE

To help you know your child more thoroughly so you can better respond to his or her needs, try the following activity. Think of the main images that filter into your child's inner-picture, his or her self-image. If your child is in the toddler to three-year-old stage, for example, your list could include these general facts: has freedom to explore, controls, much affection, and so on. Or you could be more specific and list actual activities such as: has added many new words to his or her vocabulary; moves about very much; can go all over the house if we allow it; is extremely interested in looking at magazines; carries a puppet around; will not part from a baby blanket. Be sure to include any negative as well as positive influences. If your child is five, for instance, your list could include experiences such as: still sucks thumb constantly, wets the bed at least once a week, and so on. Both positive and negative experiences affect the child's "inner-picture."

Now, write these experiences and behaviors on the blank lines radiating into the child's mirror image and identify them as positive or negative.

The experiences and behaviors you listed fit into general categories of factors radiating from experiences that help form a child's self-concept. These general categories are shown in the following diagram. Look over these factors carefully. Study them. Then rank these factors 1-8 according to their place of importance (as much as you are able to see) in your child's life. Use 1 for any factor that is extremely influential; 4 for any factor moderately so; 8 for any factor which has no influence. For example, if your child is an infant, you would, no doubt, rank "other authority—teachers and other adults" as 8.

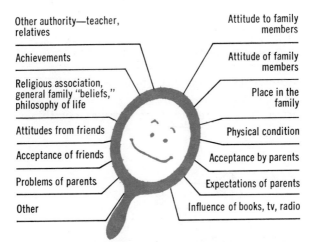

Other authority—teacher, relatives

Achievements

Religious association, general family "beliefs," philosophy of life

Attitudes from friends

Acceptance of friends

Problems of parents

Other

Attitude to family members

Attitude of family members

Place in the family

Physical condition

Acceptance by parents

Expectations of parents

Influence of books, tv, radio

Keep in mind which factors strongly influence your child's view of himself or herself. Are there factors which influence in a negative way? Now is a good time to eliminate the negative influences—as much as you are able. What strengths do you have which can eliminate these negative influences?

Keep in mind, also, that these influences will shift in importance as the child grows.

To help form your child's positive picture, reassess yourself to see how you are meeting your child's needs. In your first self-inventory, you listed those needs according to your child's age. List those needs, or any other that you might now think of, in the following chart. Then fill in your evaluation of your response to each need:

MY CHILD'S NEEDS	MY RESPONSE	HOW I SEE MYSELF		
		Good	Fair	Poor

What picture of yourself emerged from the above look at yourself? Write this in the form of a statement in the right-hand column. For example, perhaps you listed "recognition of achievements" as a need and rated your response as only fair. You may see yourself as "busy" or "preoccupied," preventing you from giving your child some of the time and recognition needed. Your statement about yourself may very well reflect your entire family atmosphere.

FAMILY ATMOSPHERE

Perhaps you remember a popular song of some years back in which a boy declared he was going to be just like his father. The lines described a growing boy's adulation of his father. And perhaps you remember the poignant ending in which the father, who had no time for his child, who always had something better to do, ruefully acknowledges that his son had indeed grown up "just like me."

The words repeatedly emphasized the importance of parent example and of family atmosphere.

Because children absorb the family atmosphere into their own lives, think carefully about the make-up of your own family atmosphere. Does it include ridicule, jealousy, hostility, put-downs, name-calling, blame, criticism, and envy, or affection, approval, praise, respect, fairness, acceptance, affection, honesty, courage, and compassion? Look over this list. Underline any of these factors moderately present in your family atmosphere. Add any factors not listed.

_____

_____

Are there more negative than positive influences radiating into your family? To help you see this, list the influences present in your family in the appropriate column on the following chart. Then select five of the most prevalent factors and list their effect on your child. Follow the examples shown.

MY FAMILY ATMOSPHERE

Positive	Negative	Effect
	put-downs	can make a child feel not worthwhile
respect		can help a child feel valued

So much of what happens in our day-by-day life goes by without any focus upon it. Thinking about the factors listed can help us see how the influence of daily habits can creep in to take permanent residence within our family. This can also help us see which "permanent resident" we might want to get rid of.

FAMILY ATMOSPHERE AND A CHILD'S SELF-IMAGE

Looking at the family atmosphere in each of the homes on the following pages and analyzing the child's needs in each of the examples can help you see how your own family atmosphere can affect your children. In the following sketches, the atmosphere of four families is reflected. Read each sketch carefully, and in the column at the right, check all of the influences which affect each of the children described. Study each influence and identify its effect as much as you are able to determine.

P (positive); N (negative); or U (unknown). (Follow the example shown at right).

	P	N	U

Jim, a six-month baby, is a wanted child. He is the third child and gets attention from his two older brothers, aged six and eight, every day after school. They go to his crib or play pen, take him out on the floor, watch him crawl, and play with him and his toys. His mother sees that he is kept clean and fed, but she is so exhausted that she really takes little extra time with him—and she feels guilty about it. She holds him very little; and, in general, lets the boys do most of the "playing" with her baby. The father's work keeps him away from home much of the time, and so extra demands are placed on the mother from her attendance at school conferences and functions to the tending to the day-by-day annoyances and necessities that come up in the family. At times, the mother feels that all she can do is drag herself around.

Joe follows in the path of a very bright sister and brother. Each is three years apart. When Joe begins school, his teachers make it apparent to him that he doesn't conform to standards of

P	N	U

performance set by his older
brother and sister. At first, he has
a happy-go-lucky attitude with his
failures and successes, and he can
even say: "I got half of my paper
wrong, Mom . . . but don't worry—
the other half was perfect!" Later,
a spirit of pushy aggressiveness
shows. His parents, realizing
what is happening, try to show
Joe that he is accepted as he is.
They wonder if they should say
anything to his teachers about
their comments and unfavorable
comparisons of Joe with his
brother and sister. But they do
nothing.

Melissa, at three, is a middle
child. She has one brother who is
in kindergarten, and a six-month-
old sister. Her mother helps out in
the kindergarten-boy's classroom,
and mother and son come home
together every afternoon.
Melissa's brother puts his papers
on the table for his dad to see
when he comes home later. The
early evenings are filled with talk
about her older brother's
accomplishments and with
watching or talking about the
baby and all of her new tricks.
Melissa likes her baby sister and
enjoys her achievements. But,
inwardly, she also resents all of
the attention to her brother and
sister. She begins to suck her
thumb much more than before.

Her parents say, "I don't know what's happening to you. All of a sudden you're a baby again."

P	N	U

Until now, **Barry's** parents thought things were going along smoothly, and they intended to keep things that way. Now, at three, their child suddenly develops fears. He begins talking of monsters "getting him," and "bad things in the dark." They say to one another, "He just isn't himself. This is perfectly foolish." They say to Barry. "Don't be silly. There's no such thing as a monster even if the neighbor children say so. Come on now. Forget it. Be a big boy!" His fears of the dark are treated with even more ridicule: "You're a smart boy, Barry. You know it's stupid to be afraid. You don't want to be stupid, do you? What possibly could happen to you? We don't want to hear any more about it."

As we look over the influences in the first example, we can see experiences that include the following apparent effects: being wanted—P; attention from brothers—P; freedom to move about—P; clean and fed—P; mother's exhaustion—N; mother's guilt—N; mother's lack of affection—N; father's absence—N or U; extra demands on mother which help make her exhausted—N or U; we also see that Jim's place in the family is an influence, but we can list that as U, for it is hard to know exactly how this affects the inner child. Despite the negative influences, the general atmosphere in the family seems to reflect love.

Looking at the family atmosphere in the second example, we see Joe's place in the family as U; for, we don't know how this affects Joe himself. We also see his acceptance of failures as P; his parents' acceptance of him as he is—P; their awareness of his pushy aggressiveness—P; the teacher's comparison with his brother and sister—N; and the parents' failure to talk to the teacher as N.

What effect do you think this family atmosphere has on Joe? _____

_____

_____

In example three, Melissa's place in the family is an unknown influence. We also see the following: little evening attention given Melissa—N; enjoyment of baby—P; inward resentment—N; parents' lack of understanding—N.

How would you rate the effect of this family atmosphere? Do you think that there are too many negative effects on Melissa to have it be more negative than positive? _____

_____

_____

Now, in the last example, we see: parents' attitude that fears are foolish—N; their ridicule of fears—N; lack of awareness that fears can be normal—N; name-calling, not listening to understand their child's needs—N; lack of real acceptance—N.

Can you see any positive influences in the last example? How would you rate the overall atmosphere here? Which of the examples of family atmosphere seemed most damaging to you? _____

_____

_____

Did any of these examples bring to mind any of your own at-home situations? They easily could have done so, for family atmosphere is such a mixture—of caring and slipping, of over-concern in some areas and not enough in other areas. It is a mixture of everything each of the selves in the family radiate upon one another simply because of their humanness. There can be no dimensions for a completely perfect family atmosphere, one that will be completely right for each of the children.

However, despite the bound-to-be imperfections, if the strange alchemy of the good and the not-so-good of each of us is blended with an overriding sincere care, the atmosphere will be such that the family members can nevertheless say, "It is good to be here."

YOUR CHILD'S INSIDE SELF: YOUR CHILD'S SELF-ESTEEM

You want to do as much as you can to give your children the fundamental inner resource of feeling worthwhile, but at times it is good to tell yourself, "I am only a person; I am not a deity." When it comes to your children's self-concept, you can do much to help form their own positive picture. But there are some things over which you have no control, other than to be aware of them and try to know each of your children and adjust your responses accordingly. But you can do much to form the outer environment that is one of the most important early influences on their inner selves. You can do much to respond to the needs that affect their inner selves.

As Rudolf Dreikurs and Loren Gray have pointed out, the outer environment (from which you respond to your children) affects their inner self, but it cannot completely control it. There are physical capacities with which your children are born; there are experiences in the children's bodies; there is each

one's special place in the family—these help form their "inner environment."

Of course, it is not how *you* view these outer and inner environments, but it is the child's own reactions to them that make up his or her true picture. You see one thing, but your children might see it in another way as it affects their own selves. Children individually assess the environments that affect them. Children carry with them their individual perspectives as they attempt to cope with life. If you could know exactly how things seem to them, it would be so much easier.

You do not know, but you can try to understand your children as much as possible. You can listen to thoughts; you can listen to feelings; you can be there with your whole self, not just physically; you can feel with them—all of this makes up the understanding that each child needs and helps give you an idea of how children feel about themselves.

Your children need to know that you are trying to know them. You can let them know you understand or try to understand by the way you talk to them and let them talk to you, by the way you listen to them and let them know you heard their words and received their feelings. They can come to know you care. And, this, in turn, affects their view of themselves.

To help you see how self-concept affects behavior, think of children or adults you know who seemingly have a poor opinion of themselves. List some of their behaviors or some of the ways in which lack of self-esteem shows itself: _____

_____

Now, think of children or adults who reflect a positive self-concept. List some of the ways by which this positive self-concept shows: _____

_____

_____

_____

Against this brief picture of the behavior of others, you can see that children who do not feel worthwhile can think, "I don't count in the world." Because of this, they may refuse to try new tasks, feeling they are incapable of success. Or, they may make impossible demands on themselves to prove they are worth something. They may display disagreeable behaviors and try to get acceptance by being bossy, rude, or obnoxious, and quarrelsome.

They may begin to think they can only be accepted by being someone who is not really there. They can thus be shaken with insecurity, a burden which can extend into the whole of their lives.

A teacher related this story about how feeling worthwhile changed the entire behavior of a four-year-old boy:

> If we praise him before he gets in the
> door, he's 100 percent better.
> Granted, a lot of what he does, the
> knocking into things, putting his
> hand in the paint, and so on, is
> accidental. But, if we praise him for
> something he has done well, even
> his accidental behavior is better.
> When his self-concept is boosted, he

really seems to be better. It's as if he is really more aware of himself in space.

He feels so inadequate at times, and he will say, "I can't do nothin' in this whole room. I just can't do nothin." And he's so much worse when he gets mad at himself.

His mother understands the situation. She's really cool, and tries to help him. One day this spring, after work, they planted a garden together. She wanted to give him the feeling of achievement in himself and the achievement in the eyes of others that would reflect back to him.

This boy's actions pointed to a principle which I have seen so often: **Children who do not find a sense of self-worth in a socially acceptable manner, can try to find it in a socially unacceptable or self-defeating way.**

Conversely, if children feel okay with themselves, they will have a realistic confidence in their abilities, their goals, and in themselves. Of course, these feelings can shift in intensity and change throughout the days, but, overall, if they are reflected most of the times in your children's lives, they will reflect happy children, children who feel worthwhile.

Which Is Your Child?

You cannot know exactly how each of your children feel inside, but when behaviors such as those mentioned above are present, you can begin to understand your child's inner picture. To help you see your child's inner idea of him- or herself, think of your child as you study the children described below and their reactions to life. After each behavior of each child, write "Most of the time," "Sometime," "All of the time," or "None of the time," as it pertains to your child (as much as you can discern).

I HAVE A POSITIVE SELF-IMAGE

1. I have confidence in what I can do and in what I cannot do. I am not over-confident nor under-confident.

_____

2. I have realistic goals and plans.

_____

3. I have a healthy, not exaggerated opinion of myself.

_____

4. Other _____

_____

_____

5. Other _____

_____

_____

I HAVE A NEGATIVE SELF-IMAGE

1. I try to gain acceptance in socially unacceptable or self-defeating ways.

_____

2. I give up and do not want to try anything new.

_____

3. I develop anxiety and feelings of insecurity.

_____

4. I think, "I don't count." I feel uncertain, inferior, dissatisfied when I compare myself with others.

_____

5. I have an unrealistic idea of my own ability and make impossible demands on myself.

_____

6. I begin to wear "masks," pretending to be someone I'm not.

_____

It is, of course, difficult to know if you have been completely right in judging how your child feels about him or herself. However, watching for these behaviors can give an indication of how a child feels about itself inside.

And, watching for these traits in your children can lead you to look closely at yourselves and ask, "What am I reflecting to my children?"

STEPS TO BUILDING SELF-ESTEEM

Respect and understanding—these are two main things you want to give to your children. They can help build their (and your own) self-esteem.

Respect and understanding are basic to any steps you can take to building self-esteem in your children. Such steps are listed in the following chart. (Because they are listed this way, do not think that there is any order in the way to follow them, or that they work independently. Real affection is present throughout all of the steps. It is not something that stands isolated.) To evaluate yourself, study the steps in column A. Then answer the questions in column B.

Do I Do This?	Yes	Most Times	Some-time	No
1. Show real affection				
2. Listen to their thoughts				
3. Listen to their feelings				
4. Provide an outlet for feelings				
5. Be realistic in expectations, and allow for failure				
6. Avoid making people feel guilty about physical characteristics, personality, or failure.				
7. Avoid insisting that good feelings should be present.				

COMMUNICATION AND SELF-ESTEEM

In this evaluation, you can see the important part communication plays in helping your children feel good about themselves. The following examples continue to show this powerful effect of communication. Each points to examples in the preceding steps and shows what not to do or say if you want to help your child feel worthwhile. Reading these examples and writing the number of the step it reflects can help you see what errors may exist in your communication patterns with your children.

a) A young mother says: When I was three, I got lost when I went to visit a friend. I can still remember how angry my dad was with me and how he drove me around and around all the area, insisting that I learn the streets and their relationship to my house. I know he really wanted to help me, but the interesting thing is, I never did get directions straight. Even as an adult, I even found it hard to read a map. I don't know if that early experience had anything to do with my ineptness at directions, but my dad sure was angry. And I was only three! *Step no. 5* (Be realistic and allow for failure.)

b) Parent to a five-year-old: Hate your brother! What an awful thing to say! Don't you ever let me hear you say anything like that again! You know you love him. *Step no.* ____

c) Parent to four-year-old: You could have done a better job than you did at cleaning up the coke you spilled in the car. Here, I had to go out and clean up after you. That's the last time you're ever going to ask for a coke when we go shopping. Now remember that! *Step no.* ____

d) Father to four-and-a-half-year-old son: Don't come crying to me about the neighbor kids calling you "Fatty." You are fat, you know. Anyway, with your size, why don't you just haul off and hit them. I'm surprised they don't call you "Sissy" as well as "Fatty". *Step no.* ____

e) Mother to four-year-old girl: I'm really surprised at you; I can't understand why you can't learn to tie your shoes. Your brother could at your age. *Step no.* ____

f) Parent to four-year-old daughter: Now, you just let your baby brother play with your music box. He's only two, and you are four. I'd think you'd want to share your things. That's being selfish. *Step no.* ____

g) Grown man: I'll never forget it. When I was a child, I was always made to kiss my aunt, and I hated it. *Step no.* ____

h) Parent to five-year-old: Now, be a good girl, and tell your sister you're sorry. You know down deep, you really are sorry, aren't you? *Step no.* ____

i) Parent to kindergarten child: What! You wet your pants! How do you think that looked in front of everyone—and in front of your little boy friend. It serves you right. You always wait too long. I've always told you that. *Step no.* ____

j) Parent of kindergarten child (very loudly, at school open house): Everyone has an apple book on his desk. You don't have any. Show me your book . . . . Well, how come you only put your first letter of your name on your apple book? Everyone else has his or her whole name written. Your know your name. You know your name don't you? Tell me, what is your name? *Step no.* ____

k) Parent at small-town bus depot as she yanks her three-year-old back in line: Stop that. What are you asking that ticket seller so many questions for? He doesn't want to be bothered with boys like you. Get over here in this line and shut up. Bad boy! *Step no.* ____

l) Parent to a 20-month-old child: If you dirty your diaper again, you're really going to get a spanking. You're just being naughty. *Step no.* ____

m) Parent (to friend): He's six months old and already spoiled. He cries whenever I leave him at his grandparents for fifteen minutes. Well, he'll just have to learn. *Step no.* ____

n) Parent to a talkative four-year-old: Stop bothering me with all that nonsense! Can't you see I'm busy. I've a hundred things to get ready for tomorrow's presentation. *Step no.* ____

If you want to check your opinions, representative answers in the list below can help you. (These are not necessarily the only steps negatively reflected.) a-5; b-7; c-5; d-6; e-5; f-3-7-4; g-7; h-7; i-6; j-1-5-6; k-5; l-5; m-5; n-7-2-3.

Even if these examples might point to what we say and do, they also show what not to say if we want to help our children feel good about themselves. They show a failure to listen to thoughts and feelings and a failure to take a realistic attitude toward errors. They make people feel guilty about their own bodily functions or personal characteristics. Through their barrage of belittling and name calling, their lack of respect and encouragement, they show how communication can reflect non-acceptance and can help shape a child.

Communication and Self-Acceptance

"Accept me as I am. Only then will we understand each other."

The young mother studied these words from a colorful poster on the wall of the Family Learning Center, and asked, "Does that mean we shouldn't want a person to change?"

"No," was the answer. "Acceptance is just the opposite. Acceptance of a person's individuality limitations, and errors, does not mean acceptance of antisocial behaviors. Acceptance means letting another know that he or she is understood, that someone is willing to listen to the other's thoughts and feelings. It is letting someone feel valued."

Acceptance does just the opposite of freezing a child into one type of behavior. It gives safety to act, to move ahead, to try out new things—to grow. Consider how we feel when we are not accepted: if we are constantly criticized for failures, we become afraid to act. For a child who has not had the chance that we have had to build a sense of identity, this can be stifling.

Acceptance can create motivation. It allows for creativity, for trying out the new in the world, and realizing the new in oneself. It provides a climate in which new tasks can be tried, new goals can be sought without fear of failure.

Acceptance is part of a real love. But acceptance of antisocial behavior, not giving a child limits, or discipline, or guidance, is the opposite of love. Acceptance of a child means accepting his or her uniqueness at each particular stage of growth and responding to accompanying needs. This response includes all of the elements of parental love. In this response you show your responsibility as a loving parent.

Nonverbal Influences In Communication

To improve your communication of acceptance, it is important to consider the deep influence all of the nonverbal things you "say" have on your child. We have already seen that from the beginning of the infant's life, nonverbal cues add immeasurably to its feeling of being a loveable and worthwhile individual. Your touches, smiles, and gestures, your tones of voice and facial characteristics start communicating immediately with your child. They "say" far more than one might think; and when they accompany words, they should convey the same message as the words. An agreeable statement with a look of displeasure only sends a mixed message to your child and results in inside confusion. The old saying: actions speak louder than words is indeed true; social scientists maintain that the nonverbal accounts for from 65% to 93% of all human communications.

Listening and Self-Acceptance

What makes you feel really good about yourself? One thing is to really be listened to, to have a friend listen to your thoughts, your words, and the feelings behind them. You know how frustrating it can be to talk with someone and feel that every time you make a statement, the other person is just waiting until you finish so he can say what is on his or her mind? And yet, don't we often do just that to our children?

To listen. To *really listen* to another person's thoughts and feelings. It sounds so simple, but to *really listen* means to listen from the other person's point of view and to let that person know you understand what he or she is saying and feeling. And it can be a very difficult thing to do—but it is one of the most powerful forces you can employ for changing and helping another. That is why listening is so vital to your children. It tells them you accept them.

Listening to your children with understanding involves trying to see their thoughts and feelings from their point of view *and* letting them know you have understood them from their own framework. You can do this by simply conveying understanding with the look on your face, by letting *them* talk and unravel feelings, and then letting them know what you think they said. Listening in this way shows your children that you care, that what they say and feel are important to you. It also gives them a chance to explain if you interpreted them correctly or incorrectly, and it gives them a chance to explain their real selves and their real feelings. If you listen in this way, you get to know your children, what they think and feel, and the things that make up their inner environment. And, in this way, you not only better know how to respond to them, but *you give them a pattern for listening to you*—and to others.

Listening truly helps in understanding the inner child and in understanding reactions to stress as the following examples show:

A two and a half year-old boy had just returned from spending a week at his grandmother's home where a traumatic family crisis occurred. Back in the quiet of his own home, he was watching a television "soap opera" with his mother, when the following dialogue resulted:

Child: Lots of bad things happen on TV, Mom, don't they?

Mother: Yes, they do. Lots of bad things.

The mother didn't interpret his remarks to her boy, just repeated them back, letting them stand in his mind the way he meant them. But she was startled when her young child immediately followed with this observation.

Child: Lots of bad things happen at grandma's house!

If the mother had not listened as she did; if she had begun interpreting the child's remark to him; if she had begun philosophizing with remarks such as, "Oh, not all the time," and tried to talk him out of his observation, she never would have been able to know what was going on inside her boy. She would not have seen firsthand how fragile a child's psyche really is. In seeing this, she is now better able to respond to him, for she knows more clearly what her boy is like. Listening with understanding helps us understand fears:

Five-year-old Amy had seen *The Wizard of Oz* on television, and so her aunt considered it a special treat to take her to see a live production. She was completely disappointed, surprised, and concerned when her niece started to huddle back in her seat as soon as the wicked witch had delivered her first speech.

Amy: Take me home. Take me home. I'm afraid. Let's get out of here.

Aunt: You're afraid of the witch.

Amy: Yes. I'm afraid. Take me home.

Aunt: You're afraid of the witch on the stage . . . You've seen this wicked witch on television in the *Wizard of Oz,* and you weren't afraid . . . .

Amy: Yes, but on television, the witch can't get out of the TV, and here she can come right down the steps and get us.

Aunt: Oh . . . I see why you're afraid. Well, she won't do that here. I know you're still afraid, but how about if we move near the door. Would you like that better? Or we can leave and not see what happens. How do you feel about it?

Amy: Well . . . let's stay, but let's stand near the door . . .

This aunt listened and accepted the child's fears. She did not deride them but presented an alternative for the child to think about. In this way, the child made the decision how to handle her fear; she saw that the witch didn't leave the stage; and she felt good about seeing the whole play.

Two-year-old Tom had to use a bathroom unfamiliar to him, a

bathroom without the security of his
small potty chair. As his mother
placed him on the toilet seat, the little
boy pleaded:
Tom: Hold me. Hold me on the seat.
Hold me.
Mother: Of course, I'll hold you.
You're afraid you're going to fall in
the toilet, aren't you?
Tom: I'm afraid I'm goin' to go down
the toilet with the water when you
flush it.

This mother, by checking out the boy's language, saw that she really didn't interpret the words correctly in the first place. This gave her boy a chance to explain how he felt and what he meant. And the mother knew the source of her child's fears—which she most likely would not have known if she had responded differently.

Four-year-old Linda would not
shut her eyes and go to sleep. Every
time her parents checked her room,
her eyes were open.
Father: Go on to sleep. You'll never go
to sleep if you keep your eyes open.
Linda: But I'm afraid to shut my eyes.
I'm afraid.
Father: You're afraid to shut your
eyes . . .
Linda: Yes. I can't shut my eyes,
because Janice told me that when
people died, they went to sleep,
and I don't want to sleep, because
then I might die.

This father did not make fun of his daughter's fears which were very real to her; he did not say "It's stupid to be afraid to shut your eyes." Instead, he listened, repeated Linda's words to her, and found the real cause for Linda's fears, a cause which was very logical to her. In this way he had a chance to talk to his daughter about death, to explain to her that going to sleep did not refer to her at all. And Linda could then better understand death. She could go to sleep without fear.

Because listening with understanding involves so very much of ourselves, it is often referred to as active listening. Similarly, listening without trying to understand what the other is feeling can be called passive listening. Because listening to, and understanding, our children plays such a vital part in our acceptance of them (and in turn, their self-acceptance), the following exercise is included.

This includes examples of both active and passive listening. You are asked to read each example and indicate what type of listening response is shown. If it is a negative response, change it to a positive one. If it is a positive response, do not change it.

> *Bob:* (Rushing home from play): Just think, Dad, the big kids asked me to play ball with them.
> *Father:* Yeah, good. Now be quiet, I'm in the middle of a program.

Type of response: _____

_____

> *Four-year-old:* None of the other kids like me. They always start to run

away when I come around. Then they start laughing and whispering together.

Mother: We all have to take our knocks in life. You're four years old now, and you should learn that nothing is easy. Besides, you probably did something that makes them act that way.

Type of response: _____

_____

Five-year-old (in phone conversation with her aunt): I'll tell you something if you don't laugh.

Aunt: No, of course, I won't laugh.

Child (lowering her voice): I had to go to the bathroom in school, and just when I got to the bathroom, I wet all my clothes. I had to go to the school secretary and tell her to call home for other clothes.

Aunt: You went to the secretary . . . and asked her to call home . . . .

Child: Yes, I didn't want to go to my teacher. I don't think she would have liked it.

Aunt: How did you feel about it?

Child: Oh, I was so embarrassed!

Type of response: _____

_____

In the first example the father definitely shows listening without understanding. This cut off further communication with his son.

The second example shows listening without understanding, listening which also includes a blaming, **you** statement: *(You* probably did something . . .")

In the third example which shows listening with understanding, the aunt really listens to the child's words and to her feelings. The child feels understood and is able to express her feelings without ridicule or put-down.

Look again at your added response for example one. Does it leave the door open for further communication?

To see how listening or not listening affects a child, imagine you are the child in each of the above situations and ask yourself, "How would I really feel?" When involved in your own parent-child talk, such putting yourself in the other's place makes for active listening and resultant feeling of acceptance in your children.

ENCOURAGEMENT, DISCOURAGEMENT, AND SELF-ESTEEM

It seems self-evident, but it is so important it must be emphasized: Not only the way you listen to your children but also the way you talk to them can affect their self-image. Encouraging or discouraging statements have a profound effect on your children's picture of themselves.

From earliest infancy, children need the satisfaction of achievements. Encouragement helps them to feel good about themselves and move on to new achievements. At first, your encouragement comes so easily. An infant's early accomplishments, first rolling over, beginning to patty-cake, or waving bye-bye are fresh and exciting. But the infant becomes a searching explorer under your feet, a toddler who is everywhere you are and everywhere you aren't. And the toddler becomes a curious three-year-old with innumerable "why's?" bombarding your every thought; then a four- and a five-year-old who wants to talk and wants to have you listen, who wants to try out new ideas and use the dining room table for new projects.

And something can happen in the process. Your children can become so familiar to you that you can take them for granted, get exasperated with them, and act as if you were thinking: "They are always with us. They know they are loved. It really doesn't matter too much what is said to them. It will rub off. They've been around us long enough to know that." And you can say things that hurt, things that you think won't matter. But they do matter; they last a long time.

Or perhaps you don't say a word but convey in verbal ways—the tone in your voice, the impatience in your gesture, or the set of your mouth that you think they are nuisances. It is so easy to forget the impact of what you don't say on children.

When somebody gives you the feeling that you can't do anything, you may feel physically and even mentally awkward, depending on how important the person is to you. Consider how children must feel if the same discouragement is given to them. Children do not have as many "important others" as you have in your life to help boost their self-esteem in other ways. You are the source of the main reflection in each child's own "inner-picture."

Discouragement can stifle a child's motivation and threaten his or her behavior. But encouragement tells children they are capable. It tells them we value their attempts and themselves. And it helps them adjust to failure.

Helping A Child Adjust To Failure

How you help your children adjust to failure depends a great deal on how you use the *language of encouragement* in their activities. If you see that your children fail in some of their attempts, try to suggest similar, but slightly less difficult projects which they can more easily master. Then let them proceed to tasks slightly more difficult. Your talk can follow patterns similar to this:

"Your stack of blocks fell down? Well, let's see if we can make two stacks of blocks with these four blocks instead of just one stack. See, we'll put one block on top of one block here. See, now we have all four blocks—and, two stacks!"

"Why are you crying? . . . Your boat always splits when you nail one piece of wood to the other? Let's see it. . . . I think if we tried again, this time using this other wood and this smaller nail, it will work. Here, let's make another."

Encouragement helps a child move ahead. Discouragement can cause a child to feel worthless and give up trying. The contrast is seen in the following statements. Read each of these, and try to imagine you are the child and that the statement is said to you. Then circle E for encouraged or D for discouraged, accordingly.

E D   **1.** To a four-year-old: I'll clean the bathroom. You just run out and play.

You'll make more trouble than it's worth.

E D 2. To a two-year-old: Hurry up, hurry up. . . . Let me do it. I don't have all day.

E D 3. To a three-year-old: I really am glad that you're helping me dry the silverware.

E D 4. To a three-year-old: Get your hands away from your face. Stop fidgeting. Listen to what I'm saying, can't you? What will I ever do with you?

E D 5. To a five-year-old: Your room is a mess. You're lazy just like your dad. You'll never grow up to be neat.

E D 6. To a four-year-old: Yes, it's okay to go over to Mary's house, but, well, I'd rather, you'd play with someone else. I don't like her mother. . . . Why? Well, you'll know when you're older.

E D 7. To a three-year-old: It's why, why, why! Go out in the kitchen and ask your mom. I'm tired of questions.

E D 8. To a four-year-old: What are you looking in the mirror all the time for? Do you think you're beautiful or something?

E D 9. To a four-year-old: I know it's not easy, but look at all you've done so far.

E D 10. To a five-year-old: You let Teddy take your tricycle, and he broke it! Why did you let him do that? Oh, don't be such a cry baby. It's your fault for letting him have it.

E D 11. To a two-year-old: I'm really pleased that you drew all those things so I

could send them to your grandmother.

E D **12.** To a one-year-old: Here, let me feed
you. You make too much of a mess.

E D **13.** To a sixteen-month-old: Watch while
I put up this other baby gate. It's sure
going to be a lot easier to block off this
room. There, now, you can have a nice
area to play in, and I won't have to
worry about you falling down the
basement steps.

E D **14.** To a two-and-a-half-year-old: Got a
little problem you say? You mean you
soiled your pants? And Jack took care
of it and threw it in the garbage! Bad
boy! Why didn't you come and tell
me? Don't ever do that again, do you
hear? I'm ashamed of you!

In going over these statements, you can see
how easy it is to slip into discouraging talk:
Examples 3, 9, 11, and 13 show encouragement. All of the others could be very discouraging to the child.

As you read these, did you notice how many
times the word "you" was used in blaming or in
labeling the child, or in general put-downs?
Can you see that the content in these messages
could have been conveyed without hurting the
child?

In talking to your children, remember: You
can say what you feel without tearing your
children down. So, if you feel hurt, or angry, or
sad, or disappointed, say so. Begin your statements with the word "I"; then say what you
see; then say how you feel about it. Take the
responsibility for your own feelings. Don't

blame your children for the way *you* feel. Consider the difference in the following.

> *First mother:* I am angry because this kitchen is such a mess.
> *Second mother:* You're really a messy girl. You said you would put the pans away if you could play with them, and then you left them all over the floor. You can't be trusted.

The first mother did not hide her feelings, nor did she let her anger cause her to begin a name-calling attack. In the second example, the mother blamed the girl, sent four accusing "you" messages, and did not take the responsibility for her own feelings.

Choose four of the discouraging statements on pages 77-79 and, using the "I" message that tells your own feelings, change them to positive statements which do not attack the child.

As you read the previous statements, did any of them reflect any of the weaknesses you listed in your first inventory? If so, don't think it is impossible to change. Work on one weakness a day at a time, and try to see some improvement within one week. Don't try to correct or change everything in your communication at once or to rid yourself of the put-down habit immediately. Make your goals realistic and attainable.

Put-Downs That Tear Down

In his booklet, *I Am Loveable and Capable,* Dr. Sidney Simon tells us that everyone wears an imaginary sign on which are written the letters—IALAC. Everyone wears such a sign, even if it cannot be seen, for the letters stand for the feeling "I Am Loveable and Capable" which is essential to all of us.

Keeping this in mind, imagine you and your child are each wearing such a sign. Now, think of all of the put-downs you yourself have received during the past week. Is that too long a time? Then shorten it to three days—or two days—or even one day. List all those put-downs you can remember.

_____

_____

_____

For each of the "put-downs" you listed, imagine yourself tearing off a piece of the sign you wear. How many pieces of your IALAC sign did you tear off? Is there much left of your sign?

Now, thinking of your child, do the same thing, imagining he or she is wearing an IALAC sign. Choose any day (or two) of the past week. List all of the put-downs your child received.

_____

_____

_____

For each of the put-downs you listed, imagine yourself tearing off a piece of your child's "I am Loveable and Capable" sign. How many pieces did you tear off? _____ Draw such an imaginary sign that represents your child.

How would it look with the pieces of himself or herself torn off? _____ Do you think if you avoid put-downs you are spoiling your child? Can you get the same message across if he or she needs discipline and correction without using put-downs?

It is vitally important that you try, for avoiding put-downs does not spoil your child, rather it avoids destruction of your child's self-esteem. Put-downs can so easily be flung out in a moment of fatigue or irritation, and they can outweigh the irritation you feel. The avoidance of them, of course, requires mentally pressing a stop-and-think button. Is pressing such a button something new to you? Then work on it one day at a time. After a week, assess any gain you may have made. Remember, any improvement is a gain. Keep focusing on those gains! Such focus can add to your strengths and to your ability as a parent.

Feelings and Self-Esteem

You listen to your children, not just to their thoughts, but also to their feelings—to know what they are like and how you can best respond to their particular needs. Helping children express their feelings in this way does more than helping you know your children. It helps them to know themselves, what is going on inside of them, and how to deal with these inside forces. Allowing them an outlet for expressing their feelings is part of helping them feel comfortable with themselves.

There is no good or bad to feelings—they are part of the human condition, and depending on how they are handled, contribute to the kind of

person one becomes. Help your children know that love and hate, happiness and sadness, pride and jealousy are part of the feelings present in all of us. Help them learn that feelings can be balanced with reason and will. Help them find socially acceptable outlets for their feelings.

"When I get angry, I play the piano," said one mother. "When I get angry, I trim away at the bushes," said another. And a father told me, "I can take out a lot of my frustrations with people when I paint a wall. I can slap away with that paint, and it really helps."

Adults have learned that it helps to have an outlet for bottled-up emotions. Children have not had the time to learn this lesson. We can help them—by providing suitable outlets for the release of these feelings.

Here are a few suggestions to help them deal with feelings in these early years:

- Talk about your own feelings and their causes from the time your children are very young. ("I am so happy that I got that telephone call from grandmother." ... "I'm really sad because I have to work tonight and can't be home with you." ...)
- "Read" picture books which show various feelings of children and adults. Discuss the feelings that are shown. Have your child "read" the pictures to you as he or she describes the feelings the pictures call to mind.
- Provide opportunities for imaginary play and games in which your child can take on other (including adult) roles.
- Allow for physical activities and play that go along with growth. Provide objects which children can climb, tug, move around. Various toys can help in releasing feelings: An inflatable toy that Johnny can "punch" and knock over can help him release emotions of anger and frustration and is a much better solution than punching his friend whenever he feels angry with him, or kicking furniture, or breaking toys with his pent-up frustration.

Above all, learn to accept what your children say as one parent did. Hanging on the wall in her office is a hand-lettered piece of paper, a note from her child. On it, the small-child printing states: "I HATE YOU NOW. BUT I'LL LOVE YOU TOMORROW."

ACTIVITIES TO BUILD SELF-ESTEEM

A child's feeling of worth is developed in daily living according to how his or her needs are met. There are, of course, no set activities required to accomplish this. But, there are things we can share with our children which can add to their feeling of worth and give them a sense of their own identity.

Some of these are common to families everywhere, games handed down from generation to generation such as Peek-a-boo (which helps a child realize he or she is separate from someone else), Patty-Cake, and This Little Piggy. There is the Where Is-Where Are . . . Game, by which children learn to identify parts of the body. (Where are your eyes? . . . your ears? . . . etc.) And there are activities such as the following which help build their identity, give them roots, and help them feel good about themselves.

Feel Wheel

Use a circle of cardboard or a large paper plate and mark off wedge-shaped areas for feelings. You can list the feelings indicated below, or any you wish. For the younger child, simply worded feelings can be used such as mad, sad, happy, and so on.

The Feel Wheel

Then print names of family members on small rectangular pieces of heavy paper and pin them to the outside of the circle. Whenever they wish, they can indicate their own feeling by pinning their name to the corresponding feeling they are experiencing. This "Feel Wheel" can be placed·in a prominent spot in your home, and even a five-year-old can use it. A younger child seeing the rest of the family showing their feelings, can also grow into its use and soon learn to "read" the feeling labels.

This idea can be adapted to different family situations. One mother of three young girls made a "Feel Wheel" weekly booklet for each of her three children. Each "Feel Wheel" contained empty wedge-shaped areas. The two older girls, 6 and 9, printed in their feelings each night. The youngest child, a 5-year-old, told her feelings to an older child or to her mother, and then these feelings were printed in. In their individual "Feel Wheels" they said such things as "Mad at Mom," "Mad at Sandy," "Happy with Mom," and even "Mad at my feet."

Family Photo Album

Print the words "Our Family" on a photo album. Let your children help you place family pictures in it. Write the names of family members under each picture. Then let your child go through the album and identify the pictures. The activity can delight a child even as young as 16 months. And, of course, it can be adapted and modified as the child becomes older.

All About Me Booklet

You can help your child construct an "All About Me" booklet. You can use construction paper, wrapping paper, typing paper, or whatever, for the pages, and these pages can be punched and laced or stapled together. Depending on the child's age, this can be filled with pictures your child cuts out, with his or her own art, or "writing." Use your imagination for titles that focus on a child's individuality: "Things I Like To Eat," "I Like . . . ," "Friends I Would Like to Have," "What I Want to Be When I Grow Up," and so on. Give your child water colors, crayons, or washable marking pens for his or her own endeavors.

Family Sharing Chart

Make a chart like the one shown below. List the responsibilities of the various family members. Allow a space near the chart for happy faces on which are printed the different family members' names. Let your children draw in a happy face for each responsibility accomplished. At the end of the week, if the majority of responsibilities have been accomplished, let them place a happy face in the end column. This helps them learn to assess themselves.

Our Family Sharing Chart

Name	Task	Sun	Mon	Tues	Wed	Thurs	Fri	Sat	My work
	Dusting								
SALLY	Making bed								
	Setting table								
STEVE	Picking up papers								
SANDY	Straightening toys—night								
	Emptying Wastebaskets								
MIKE	Feeding dog								
	Sweeping porch								

Family Wall

Make a picture grouping on the wall of your home. It should include pictures of the immediate family, relatives, and, if possible, ancestors, so your children can have a sense of belonging to a wider family than that in their own home.

Special Places

If possible, create a special place in your home which each child can call his or her very own—even if this special place is a corner of a room, or a shelf for toys and possessions. Individual places can be decorated with individual art work or ideas. If there is little space in your home, try giving each child a box that fits under the bed. These can be individually decorated with pictures cut from old magazines or by "painting" with felt-tipped pens. (Use pens with washable ink or washable painting materials.)

Show your children how to draw a simple floor plan of your home. Color a favorite room with a marking pen. Then, have your children do the same thing. Have them tell you about their favorite room.

Your Childhood Home

If possible, take them to your first home. If this is not possible, talk to your children about your first home. Tell them words you associate with your first home. Ask them what words they can say to tell you about their home. This can help them see their home as a sheltering and nurturing place and to see the similarities or difference between their feelings and yours. Accept, without shaming, any possible negative comment; this helps show children they themselves are accepted. In this way, they will be more likely to accept your own individual views.

Poster Selves

Make outlines of your children on wrapping paper, cut them out, and place the "posters" on the door or wall of their rooms. Identify each of the "posters" with each of your children's name. They can cut out pictures of favorite things to attach to "themselves." Similarly, have them cut out examples of people showing different feelings. Whenever they have a feeling similar to any in the pictures, they can attach their "feeling pictures" to their individual poster.

Family Song

Make up a family song, or a friends' song, using names and one identifying trait. ("I have a friend, Annie, who lives next door . . .")

Home Stories

Have your child tell you a story about your home. As he or she tells the story, you can write it in a homemade book of paper pages stapled together. Title it MY HOME by _____ (print your child's name).

Happy Stories

Play (listing reasons) an "I Am Happy with Me Because . . ." game, each alternating in listing reasons.

Individual Times

To help each child in your family feel important, you can follow this example of a young single parent who has the custody of her three young children. To add to their individual security, she lets each of them alternate in choosing one activity a month to share alone with her without the others. The children's choices are simple, but this is an excellent time for them to tell the mother things they do not want the others to know. It helps each child feel special.

Do I Agree? Do I Disagree?

Now, after looking at various activities to share with your child, here is an activity you can enjoy alone. The following statements are based on the material previously covered; they are designed to stretch your thinking, to help you examine more precisely the place of self-esteem in your child's life. There are no right and wrong answers as such.

Your task is to read each statement, then circle A if you agree or D if you disagree with each statement. If you wish to change the wording in a particular statement so that you can circle A, do so. This is also a good activity to share with a partner or in small group situations. In the latter, try to come to an agreement by changing the wording so that you can agree. If you can't agree, agree to disagree. Accept and keep thinking about each other's views.

A D **1.** Children who do not receive proper affection and a sense of self-worth from their home will accomplish less than they might have.

A D **2.** The need for love and the need to feel worthwhile are present in some people from birth until they are adults.

A D **3.** The mark of an expert parent is to have a child who shows a great amount of self-confidence.

A D **4.** Saying, "I love you" over and over will give a child a sense of feeling valued.

A D **5.** One positive experience of a child will balance one negative experience.

A D **6.** Listening to our children is more important than talking to them.

A D **7.** The pressures of associates and friends is as important to a kindergarten child's self-concept as the influence of parents.

A D **8.** To understand our children is easy.

A D **9.** Nonverbal language always has more effect on a child than verbal language.

A D **10.** Even if a child does not feel loveable and worthwhile, he or she can succeed.

A D **11.** A child always feels good about himself or herself if he or she has a positive self-concept.

A D **12.** Teachers will correct a low self-image in children when they begin school.

A D **13.** We listen to our children because it is necessary to understand them at all times.

A D **14.** Children will feel loved without your telling them you love them.

Throughout the following days think about these statements. Ask yourself, "Is my thinking changing because I am giving myself some time to let my thoughts grow?"

CHANGE AND GROWTH

As you have worked through the previous section which focused on the part you play in helping your children feel good about themselves, in what way did your image of yourself as a parent change? To help see any such changes, go back to your self-inventory which preceded this section. Again, study this carefully. Record any changes in yourself in the space below according to the suggestions shown.

I am: (more confident, less anxious about perfection, etc.)

_____

_____

_____

Remember that any change means growth and that this growth in you will probably be reflected in your child. Remember that growth means a continual beginning.

To help you along your way in this new beginning, here is the personal experience of a young mother, who, during a busy day, took time to listen and to accept the feelings of a small daughter. It exemplifies how you can help your children when they begin to doubt themselves.

> "I wish, oh I wish, I wish I were like Sally . . . or Jane . . . or Mary," this child would say to her mother on those occasions when the special attributes or possessions of others seemed so alluring; when another person's clothes, or beauty, or whatever seemed so much more shining than her own.
>
> The mother listened, and then replied, "If you had to change everything you are for everything Sally is . . . or Jane . . . or Mary, would you trade everything?"
> "Everything?" the child would ask.
> "Everything?" That was quite a trade.
> "No, I wouldn't want to trade *everything* I have for everything someone else has. No. I'd rather be me. I'm glad I'm me."

"I'm glad I'm me!" That's what self-acceptance is all about. That's what feeling worthwhile is all about. Four words, but four words that can influence an entire lifetime, "I'm glad I'm me."

section
3

Creativity

I have spread my dreams under your feet;
Tread softly because you tread on my dreams.
W. B. Yeats

With their inner urge to grow, children who feel happy with themselves keep wanting to learn, to find the new in the world—and in themselves. This is discovery, and it is part of the creativity of young children.

The creativity of young children—that brief phrase unveils a wealth of pictures. There is the three-year-old sailing a boat in new puddles of water after a spring rain, the two-year-old making a grassy home for a lightning bug in a glass jar, or spreading out flat in the bathtub and saying, "I'm a turtle," the four-year-old setting a table for an imaginary family of dolls, the toddler stacking a wavering tower of blocks to a childhood sky.

We have all seen real-life pictures like these—and many more. Young children are naturally creative as they try themselves out on the world that is so new to them. In varying ways they are seeking to discover more about themselves and more about the places around them. In their unclouded vision, all in fresh, untouched. They are learning a sense of wonder from this world, from what they can do in it, and how they can affect it. And as they meet the challenge of interacting with the world, they are discovering themselves. In a very real sense, they are creating themselves.

Children's play is not just recreation but a continual "re-creation" vital to their development.

Watching children at play, you see this "re-creating;" you see creativity, the products of its expression, and the elements that contribute to it. But as you watch this early childhood play and become fascinated with its activities, a variety of questions occur—questions related

to how you can best foster this creative development and keep it alive in the face of society's pressure for conformity. And so the questions present themselves:

- What really is creativity?
- Why is its development vital to a child's entire life?
- What is the link between self-esteem and creative expression?
- What is the link between the development of creative experiences and learning?
- How can you foster creativity and learning in these early years?
- How do you stifle creativity and learning?

Exploring the answers to these questions is what this section is all about.

Before beginning this exploration, stop to examine your own feelings about the creativity of children and your part in developing it. This time of reflection and recording of your own reactions can give you a better personal perspective in viewing your role in nurturing children's creative expression. If there is anything you cannot answer, don't be concerned; responses and further insights can come to you as your progress through the pages that follow.

CREATIVITY: A SELF-INVENTORY

1. How do you define creativity? _____

   _____

   _____

   _____

2. List traits common to creative expression: _____

   _____

   _____

3. Do you want your child to be creative?

   _____

   Why or why not? _____

   _____

4. What traits do you have which can help develop creativity in your child? _____

   _____

   _____

   _____

5. Is there a link between fostering creative expression and fostering learning? ____

_____

Explain. _____

_____

6. What are some of the things you do now to develop creative expression in your child? _____

_____

_____

7. What are some of the things you do now which might stifle creativity in your child? _____

_____

_____

8. What strengths do you have which can help develop your child's creativity?

_____

_____

_____

When you attempted to define creativity, did you find it difficult? Did the elusiveness of the word make you draw a hazy-edged picture in your mind? Despite what was said earlier about the creativity in all children, do you tend to think of creativity as only a special artistic ability such as painting a beautiful picture or composing a poem? It can be that, of course. But creativity as we are talking about in this section is not limited to only those special talents of the artist. The creativity we refer to is more encompassing.

Creativity is the ability to make or to find the new. It is being able to experience a part of life in a way not previously experienced. Whether seeing something in a new light or figuring out an answer to a problem or "making something," creativity changes our being. It expresses ourselves. When we are creative, something happens inside of us, and something happens outside of us. Creative experiences help enlarge us: inside of us we feel the stirrings of achievement.

Which of these added statements about creativity is (are) most meaningful to you? Check the one (ones) important to you.

_____**1.** Creativity is the discovery of something about oneself in relationship to the world around us.

_____**2.** Creativity is the taking of "what is" to "what might be possible."

_____**3.** Creativity is the making of the new.

_____**4.** Creativity is doing in one's unique way what is self-enlarging.

_____**5.** Creativity can be both process (what is "going on inside of us") and product (what is created): what is going on inside of us at the time of creation and what happens inside us as we view a product of our creation.

As you could see, there is no *one* right statement here that sums up what creativity really is. It could be that you found all statements important to you—for each expresses something of what happens in a creative act. But, there is much more; these statements form only a framework for creativity and its importance in giving meaning to our lives.

CREATIVITY AND SELF-ESTEEM

In analyzing creativity in your child, let us see what happens inside all of us when we create.

Creativity helps us discover something about ourselves we did not know before. If we paint a picture, gain a new realization with a sudden flash of insight, or plan a creative answer to a problem, we have added another dimension to ourselves. Creativity extends us, and, in seeing this extension, we feel more confident, surer of our value. It is a reaffirmation of ourselves to know that we have brought this new thing (whether it is an idea, realization, game, plan, or intricate structure) into being.

Let us look at various aspects of creativity. It can be the *inside* realization of something not realized before. It can be that flash of light that bursts inside you as this occurs. It can be what happens inside of you, as "maker," joining with what you brought to existence.

The fact that you have experienced this helps you learn more about yourself and what occurs inside you. In seeing something in a new light, what you have newly experienced takes on a different relationship to the world than it had before. For creation involves more than yourself. It is you interacting with some part of what is around you.

In the creative expression that results when insight couples with activity to produce a visible product of change, you are also changed. This occurs whether you write a story, compose a poem, concoct a special recipe, or devise a new room arrangement. You have experienced that you can make new, that you have a power to change something into what was not present before. In seeing this newly created expression of yourself, you realize that you have been changed; it is you who have added this new existence to the world.

Focusing on your own creativity can help you know something about the creative expression of children. Remember what was said in the preceding section about achievements adding to children's forming a positive picture of themselves:

- Achievements are components which add to self-acceptance, the feeling that "I am O.K."
- Helping a child achieve this self-acceptance, this positive self-esteem, is one of the most important things we can give our child.
- Positive self-esteem affects a child's entire present. It affects a child's future.

Achievements realized in creativity thus are vital to a child's life.

Children who are basically confident, who feel good about themselves, are free for further creative ventures. They are not afraid to try new things. They are free to let their imagination soar, to let their curiosity seek out new experiences; they are free to fail. And, in being free to fail, they are free to try again and achieve. Self-esteem and creativity reinforce each other.

Think of the various images that reflect into your child's inner-picture. Think how achievements are vital to the formation of positive self-esteem. In the mirror image below, list the achievements *your child* realizes in creative play or endeavors which can radiate to a positive inner picture, to self-esteem.

Creative Achievements and Self-Esteem

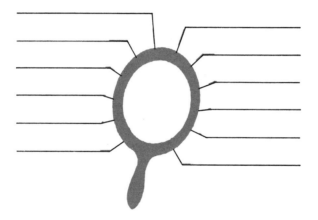

Remember that these achievements are part of *all* achievements which help form children's positive pictures of themselves.

Whether making a city in the sand-pile, a design with crayons and paper, or playing doctor using their dad's necktie for a stethescope, such play is helping children feel happy with achievement—and happy in trying out adult roles as they go about their play.

As you watch your children intent upon such play, think how such continued satisfactions radiate into their inner-picture of themselves.

The Importance of Play
in Creative Experience

Have you ever watched a group of children tugging boxes to build a house, seen their persistence, determination, pride in accomplishment and satisfaction? Or have you seen a group of three-year-olds playing house, or four-year-olds dressing up in adult clothes to become an entirely new family? Have you watched children in imaginative, dramatic play engaged in the make-believe of other worlds? Or have you watched them playing with puppets? If so, you could see in these types of play children developing inner resources vital for future growth. These children were:

- Being independent, setting up their own rules.
- Learning to cooperate with one another according to the new rules they devised along the way.
- Making decisions.
- Changing decisions as they thought necessary.
- Learning to get along with other children.
- Learning to share responsibilities.
- Trying out adult roles.
- Learning to accept and work with change.
- Learning that failure can provide an opportunity to try again in another way. Learning that failure can give an opportunity to work out a better solution to a problem.

Recently, I observed a group of handicapped preschoolers building a dump out of large cardboard building blocks. It was before school time, and their regular teacher was not present. They would construct a fortress of a wall, take it down, reconstruct it, work together *without* adult direction on what was their own decision. *Without* adult direction at this particular time, they were actively demonstrating the qualities of inner growth. Whether in such group play or in individual creative experiences, the child is taking charge, not sitting

idly by, passively being molded by the environment.

Think of your own children and their creative play. Remember that such play is not just passing time but part of developing themselves. It can help develop some or all of these inner resources: independence, hope, freedom to fail, cooperation with others (including cooperating with the rules of others); and it can develop the ability to solve problems, to find new solutions, to make decisions, and to deal effectively with change.

Play does not have to be out of the ordinary to develop these inner resources. The following few examples show types of very ordinary play with which we are all familiar. Look at these examples of creative play and write the resources such play develops in the second column.

Creative Play	Inner Resources Developed
Making cakes with play dough	Independence, making decisions, freedom to fail
Making towns and cities in a sandbox	
Building cities out of playing cards	
Making a toy out of a shoe box and a piece of string	
Finger painting	
Shaping a set of dishes with clay	
Playing school	

What inner resources did this help you discover in your children? Independence? Getting along with one another? Willingness to take risks? You can learn a lot about your children's perspective of themselves as you watch them at play. You can better respond to them with a deepened awareness of their individuality, realizing that, as Martin Buber has expressed it, "Every person born in this world represents something new, something that never existed before, something original and unique."

Creativity and Change

Today's children live in a jet-spanned, fast-moving world where far-reaching changes take place within brief spans of time. Through television they view changes affecting the entire universe in the dimensions of their own living room.

How will they cope with this change that is so much a part of their life today? Remember, it is predicted that the average young adult today will change careers five times in his or her lifetime. What about today's children as they become tomorrow's adults? Will a handed-down set of rules, values, "goals-that-are-good" told to them in one era serve them for all time?

Or will they be better served by learning to make changes in themselves as necessary, but have the confidence not to change if they so choose, by learning to reassess themselves in a continuous process of growth?

The experiences and skills creative play develops in childhood—independent thought, curiosity about new solutions, realization that failure allows them to try again, and that they have the power to change their environment, decision making, getting along with others, figuring things out—are all important for coping with both the present and the changing future.

The beginning child finds himself or herself in interaction with a world that is all new. As this world becomes more familiar, he or she absorbs countless impressions and develops life-giving inner resources. You as a parent can help your children meet this world in a way that keeps the creative urge alive within them.

The impact of these early experiences is expressed well in the reflections of an adult friend who has survived a number of misfortunes:

> I have really had some terribly hard knocks in life, but, I always bounced back. I always felt that there was a solution if I looked hard enough, that if I searched enough or if I looked at things in a new way, there could be an answer.
> As I analyze this, I give my mother a lot of credit for instilling in me this "Jack-in-the box" ability to bounce back. I remember her zest for life, her imaginative way of looking at things, even when I was very young. I remember *the games she played while going about her household routine, her allowing me to try out new ideas and sharing with me a continual search for new things and yet also instilling in me a satisfaction with what we had at hand.* In fact, we often *had* to use what we had at hand in order to make something new. And, in all of this, if, at times things didn't work out or we couldn't find a better solution, there was the realization that at least we tried. I guess what was so good about it all was that it allowed me to *hope* and to know that *I* could do something to bring about what I hoped for.

Hers is a testimony that any parents can look to as they help pattern their child's future. You can see the development of another inner resource here: the link between creative endeavor and the inner resource of *hope*.

Creative Experiences and the Steps to Learning

To foster the inner resources that creative experiences can develop, let us first look at the steps involved in creative expression. Then let us consider these steps and their relationship to your child's learning process.

What happens in a creative experience?

First, there is an awareness and observation. With this, or following it, are independence and freedom, curiosity, imagination, freedom to fail, and further awareness or observations. One can call these the components of creative experience. They are present when the child first sees a part of his world and acts upon this awareness. Something goes on inside of him similar to this:

> (Independence and Freedom, Curiosity, Imagination) AWARENESS   I CAN ACT ON THIS AWARENESS.   I ACT. I AM CHANGED. (Further awareness)   (If I fail, I can repeat the cycle).   AWARENESS   I CAN ACT ON THIS AWARENESS. I ACT. I AM CHANGED.

Awareness and observation, independence, curiosity, imagination, freedom to fail—this is what makes up a creative experience. Looking at these *parts of creativity,* we can see the link between creativity and learning.

To help see this more clearly, study the chart below. Read column A, and, following the example in column B, list one example of creative play of your child in column C to show how learning also occurs. (Complete each step in column C).

A	B	C
Components of creativity and steps to learning	**Child thinks/ feels/learns**	**Child thinks/ feels/learns**
Playing with clay		Your example: playing with _____ _____
Awareness and observation	I see something which is soft and squishy.	I see _____ _____
Independence and freedom	I **can try** to make something from this.	I can try _____ _____
Curiosity	**What** shape can I **make?**	What can I _____ _____
Imagination	I can make a plate.	I can _____ _____
Freedom to fail	It doesn't look like a plate. (Or: It is a plate.)	It _____ _____
Making further observations (Creative thinking)	**This can** be shaped again. Maybe I can shape it into a cup. Or I can make cookies with it. Further awareness I **am** changed.	This can _____ _____ I am changed. ____

As you watch your children at play, think of this relationship between creativity and learning and enjoy the adventure in following the expansion of creativity and learning in them.

FOSTERING CREATIVE EXPRESSION IN YOUR CHILD

Sensory Experiences

From their very first days, children are reaching toward independence. They want to know, to be, to discover.

You as a parent can do much to keep that early creativity alive and to develop it by helping your children develop sensory awareness. You can instill in them a pattern for a continual sense of wonder, in the world, its people and objects, by communicating a joy in discovery, a joy in continual learning. These are the years you are setting the pattern for their life.

We are not talking about teaching your child to be a famous pianist or a talented artist, but in simply (but profoundly) helping your child be alert to the possibilities that exist within and about. You, the assistant architects of these early years, can help develop the components of creativity and learning. *You can do this by offering and allowing a wide variety of experiences. But offer and allow these experiences—don't force them upon your child.*

All of these experiences can help later reading and understanding come alive. They help your child grasp variations in letters, sounds, shapes, and rhythm of words, and structure of sentences. These experiences are stored inside of your child to add invaluable richness of meaning to words, to ideas, to life.

Everything comes to children through their senses. They learn about themselves and the world by feeling cold ice cubes melt through their fingers, by seeing how water moves when they step in it, by feeling it between their toes, by feeling and seeing sand slip through their fingers, by the feel and sight of swirling finger paints on smooth paper, by hearing thunder, by tasting a cookie or crayon, by hearing the sounds of a rattle and seeing and feeling a colorful wall hanging by their bed, by hearing the chirp of the birds or the roar of a jet plane overhead, by smelling baby powder or simmering coffee, by using their voices in first infant

cries and in early syllable formation of words, and then in the more complicated vocabulary of a three-year-old.

Seeing, tasting, smelling, hearing, touching—the world comes to children so magnificently—but so simply. Through the senses, children take from the world—and add to themselves. The more they know of the world, the more they discover of it—the more associations they can make as they relate experiences to new experiences to form the birth of new thoughts.

This does not mean you should push your children into learning beyond their capacity or subject them to so many stimuli that they cannot absorb any one experience fully enough to have it mean anything to them. It means to allow your children to *experience* the world, *to let them take the time to observe and to really absorb what they have observed.*

So, introduce your children to the world. Tell them about this world. From the very first days of their life, *talk to them, hold them, love them.* They will feel the warmth of your love, hear the nuances in the shadings of your voice and the formation of syllables they hear you use. They will begin to be aware of the way certain things you say make you feel inside by watching your smiles, your laughter, your frowns.

Let them see that you are glad to share the world with them. Recite nursery rhymes and poetry to them. They will begin to absorb the sound of the words and the rhythm of their message. They will begin to feel the pulsations of rhythm inside of themselves. As they grow, give them attention while they begin to sway to the music, to dance to the records on the record player or to the music on radio or television or to your singing while you are preparing a family meal. Allow them freedom to express the rhythm of life around them as they grow and become able to use their body to run, to jump, to spread out like a turtle, or curl up like the letter "C."

As they reach the questioning of the two-year-old stage, answer their questions to keep curiosity alive. And ask them questions of your own. In the continuing preschool years, keep their imagination alive by playing imagination games, games that help them pick out colors, listen to sounds, and find shapes and lines and curves—the horizontal lines of the telephone wires, the vertical lines of the telephone poles, the curve of the hills. Help them discover. *And then, don't crowd. Let them discover things by themselves.* Give them time alone to find out by themselves. That is where they can feel the joy of solitary achievement. But be there when they want to share their discoveries with you.

The joy of discovery begins early. The following few examples focus on everyday experiences and how they help stimulate the senses to become part of the learning process. They show again that early experiences do not have to be out-of-the-ordinary to be valuable in developing creativity and learning.

Read these suggestions in column A. In column B, write the senses being developed (as indicated in the example). Add examples of your own children's activities and the senses developed accordingly.

A	**B**
To Stimulate Creativity and Learning	**Through These Senses**
(Infant-toddler ages)	
Use a musical crib mobile above crib	sound, touch
Sing lullabies	_____
Provide soft, cuddly toys	_____
According to their age, talk about the different textures of their food.	_____
(Toddler to three-year-old)	
Provide boxes and blocks	_____
pans to stack	_____
colorful containers for toys	_____
clay, play dough, paint	_____
(Three through five-year-old)	
Provide nails and hammer, wood—and "watchfulness"	_____
various sizes of old keys to place on hooks on a board	_____
boxes	_____
jigsaw puzzles with large pieces	_____
(Three through five-year-old)	
Wall hanging with various pockets and a variety of objects—large and small, various colors and shapes that can help show opposites, colors, sorting out games.	_____

Keep thinking of other ways to stimulate learning. Use your imagination. Feel the sense of curiosity in what goes on about you. Be enthusiastic, independent in your way of seeing things, in your sense of discovery. Your children will catch your enthusiasm, your sense of finding the new in a familiar world. They can feel your radiance and learn that it, too, is for them—and all free—only for the reaching.

ACTIVITIES TO STIMULATE CREATIVITY AND LEARNING

Creativity can be nurtured by offering children a variety of sensory experiences. Here are suggestions of things you can do to enlarge these beginning experiences. As in all of this book, do not think that all of the suggestions

must be followed, or that these are the "best" things which can be enjoyed with your child. Rather take these ideas as a starting point. You will probably soon develop ideas of your own that you may find more appealing or suitable to your situation.

Study the examples in each box; then below the list of suggestions, write activities of your own which you would like to experience with your child.

To Develop the Sense of Hearing, Parents Can:

- Sing to their infants, not just when rocking them to sleep, but in their awake hours.
- Give toddlers spoons and a pasteboard box to beat rhythm.
- Play listening games.
- Crumple a sheet of paper or aluminum foil.
- Put buttons, sand, or coins in three film cans, and have your children guess the different sounds.
- Ask, "How does the furnace sound? How does the running water sound? A car sound?, etc."
- Play a "Close Your Eyes and Listen" game, each of you alternating naming all the things you hear.
- Talk about the differences in sounds; teach them songs—to sing along with you or with songs on the record player.
- Help children see how through imaginative games and acting out nursery rhymes, poetry, fairy tales, or their own stories, they can imitate the sounds of different voices—and even the sounds of animals.

To Develop the Sense of Hearing, I Can:

_____

_____

_____

To Develop the Sense of Smell, Parents Can:
- Take time to help your children notice the various scents of flowers, of weeds, of vegetable leaves, of common foods around the house, of different spices, of pepper, salt, coffee, etc.
- Play a blindfold game: Have them guess the scent of any of the above.

To Develop the Sense of Smell, I Can:

_____

_____

_____

To Develop the Sense of Taste, Parents Can:
- Remember that one of children's earliest experiences is tasting. They literally put almost everything in their mouth, so watch them with care. Talk to them about the differences in the food they are eating.
- As they grow older, use adjectives to describe various foods: _hot_ vegetables; _cold_ milk, _soft_ potatoes; _salty_ crackers, _delicious_ ice cream, _sweet_ candy, _bitter_ chocolate, _sour_ lemon, etc.
- Ask them to describe to you what they are tasting.

To Develop the Sense of Taste, I Can:

_____

_____

_____

To Develop the Sense of Sight, Parents Can:

- Go through magazines and help your children find familiar objects. Talk about these pictures and about items in catalogues. Ask them to tell you the differences and similarities between items.

- Play games such as "How Many Things Are in this Room?" or "What Was in the Picture?" each closing your eyes and naming as many things as you can remember seeing. Place items on a tray, and play the same game.

- Make trips discovery times. Whether walking to the grocery store or traveling to visit their grandparents, discuss the various things you see: the cracks in the sidewalk, the pussy willows in the spring; the icicles hanging from roofs, and the frost on the windowpanes of the houses, the trucks with their various colors and letters, and the cars of the train that pass slowly while you are waiting to cross the track. When you return home, play games of "How Many Things Can You Remember?" each taking turns in stating "things remembered."

- From three on (or thereabouts) you can help them find opposites (little-big; tall-short; fat-thin) of things they see.

122

To Develop the Sense of Sight, I Can:

_____

_____

_____

To Develop the Sense of Touch, a Parent Can:

- Crumple up different types of paper: aluminum foil, tissue paper, paper towels . . . and have your children feel the differences and tell you about them.
- Talk about the feel of different objects: *cold, smooth* ice cubes, the *hard* wood table, the *soft,* padded chair, the smooth *cool* glass of milk, the *hot* coffee cup, the *soft,* fuzzy mittens, and the *hard,* leather soles of shoes.
- Blindfold your children and have them identify objects on a tray by touching them: a button, a piece of fabric, various sizes of coins, a block and so on.

To Develop the Sense of Touch, I Can:

_____

_____

_____

You can see that there are innumerable ways to develop your children's learning through the senses. Many of these suggestions can be enjoyed spontaneously as part of your family living.

Do not think that these, or similar activities, are tagged with a "For Mothers Only" sign. Similarly, do not think that being a single

parent or a parent employed away from home will keep you from engaging in these activities. Busy fathers, mothers, single parents— are constantly demonstrating just the opposite. They know that in helping children learn from the world, they are also "making a living" for them.

FOR PARENTS TO CREATE: A CLIMATE OF CREATIVITY

It can hardly be stressed enough—a climate of affection and acceptance helps foster creativity. Children who feel accepted will feel a freedom to express themselves. This freedom is important for creative expression, but, as we noted in the preceding section, freedom does not mean lack of control. Acceptance does not mean a smothering attention. A balance must always be kept in mind.

Creative expression allows for expression of feelings. This, in turn, helps free children of burdensome troubles. Angers, fears, worries—these can be loosened by providing creative outlets: the use of clay, paints, water, and sand to manipulate, to blend, to move, to control. As you watch your children in their creative expressions, you can learn more about them and their needs. Accept what they tell you about their feelings or creative endeavors without criticism.

Avoid saying "Draw only happy things," or "Why do you paint as if your are angry?"

Avoid saying, "Let me show you a faster way of doing this," or "*This* is the way you draw smoke, not the way *you* are doing it."

Avoid saying, "That doesn't look like a man to me. It looks more like a fish." These criticisms can stifle creativity—and close communication. Accept your children's creative expressions, and you will learn more about them.

It takes very little to instill in children this sense of discovery, of wonder, and of learning to keep alive the creativity that is innately theirs. Sincere interest in them as individuals, time for you to show this interest, time for them to discover freedom of space and place, time to work/play/create with—these make up a climate of creativity—these can be a part of everyday living. They can be free to us, and they can give our child a wealth of inner resources for life.

From You: Your Interest and Time

In the climate of acceptance and affection, you can keep creativity alive by letting your children feel your interest in what they are doing. You can take time from your thoughts and activities to help show them what is around them, to help them to discover. You can take time to listen to them when they want to share their own discovery with you.

At this time, you may think, "Take time to share with my child! I have no time to spare. I have all I can do to keep my job, and I have to keep that or they won't even eat!"

The time suggested here does not have to be all the time, or even a great deal of time, just *enough* time. Such time can be time when you are taking them to, or picking them up from, the sitter, or on weekends, or when you are preparing the meals, or driving to the store, or getting them ready for bed. (It has already been stressed that these activities aren't meant for only at-home parents, but it is so important that it bears repeating.) Busy parents emphasize this fact:

- A mother of two preschool children with a middle-of-the-day lecturing job taking time to attend toy-lending workshops for preschool parents, playing games with her three-year-old son to help teach color, size, shape, and sequence.
- Fathers with very demanding schedules that take them away from home many evenings taking time to play learning games with their children.
- A mother of four, providing them with a homemade table (formica-covered wood on

squatty legs) in the corner of a room on which various creative supplies—paper, paints, marking pens, clay are readily available.

- A busy secretary, a single parent, whose work demands overtime hours, talking to her three-year-old daughter while taking her to and from work, taking time to sit on the steps with her child to talk about the sky, the clouds, the trees—all the discoveries around her.

These parents exemplify *all parents* who show that time and interest make precious gifts to our children, and that this can be given despite busy days.

It is this time and interest that lead a child to the unfolding world and all that can be learned in it.

Remembering that awareness and observation are the first steps in a creative (and learning) experience, take time to answer your children's questions, to ask questions about what they are doing and about things you are doing. Take time to help them notice life around them—the flowers poking their heads above the ground, the design of the sidewalk that leads to the grocery store. Take time to ask how the snow feels on their face, what the jet trail in the sky reminds them of, what they would be doing if they were a father, a mother, a policeman, a bus driver, a carpenter, a teacher . . . .

Don't worry that you are required to carve out an extra chunk of time. Just work into the time you have, whatever you can do that will help them be aware of life. Almost any time is the right time for helping them notice the new roof on the neighbor's garage, the garden just planted, the fence the man across the street is installing, the building being torn down, the apartment house being remodeled. If you live in an area where it is impossible to see such activities, look at magazines and talk to them about the pictures.

Take Time to Be With Your Children, and Give Your Children Time to Be Alone by Themselves—to Discover What They Can Find Alone: time to discover how the wind feels against their face when they run, time to work in their room on a project of their very own, time to plan. Give your children time by avoiding overregimentation. Don't pack their days so full of various activities that they have no time for wonder or imagination or for just figuring things out. Give them time to just "be." This also helps them discover themselves.

Stimulate, don't overwhelm. Too much stimulation can blanket true observation and awareness, so necessary for any creative experiences. For, in observing and in being aware, children need time and freedom to internalize what they are observing. Watching young children shows us how they draw into themselves everything they observe: how they take out the last piece of ice left in the glass, hold it, pick it up if it falls on the floor, examine it. How a scrap of paper on the floor or the tiniest piece of cookie on the table is held and intensely examined. How the plastic fruit is tasted, how the most minute detail is deeply absorbed. Smothering a child with too many stimuli does not allow for such observation. It does not allow for such awareness. It can still the imaginative process.

As a parent, you might well question, "But doesn't an active imagination in my children mean that they will be unproductive, caught in fantasy life of day dreams?"

Actually fantasy and make-believe appear to produce just the opposite. Jerome Singer observes that "children whose games are poor in make-believe and fantasy are likely to have trouble recalling and integrating the details of events they hear about." Singer emphasizes that research indicates that independence, peacefulness, and a realistic grasp of events can result from a "well-developed fantasy life."

A fantasy-life and imagination are not to be feared but to be fostered. The question to ask now is: "What can I do to accomplish this? How can I help my child develop the components of creativity?" Stop and examine your individual life pattern to help give you the answer. Then record your own future action below.

To Help Develop Awareness, Observation, Curiosity, Imagination, Independence, and the Freedom to Fail, and Further Awareness, I Can Take Time to

_____

_____

_____

I Can Allow Them Time of Their Own By _____

_____

_____

Does what you have recorded about yourself show that such time can be blended in with other things you are doing—that you can take time to watch your children paint, for instance, or listen to your child while he holds two bananas together to make a circle and then says, "This looks like a funny O," that things such as this can be done while you are preparing a meal or straightening up the house? Do you see that allowing your children time of their own means not overcrowding their day, that giving such time uncrowds their mind, and, that, like uncrowded plants, children's minds can flourish when not overattended.

For Them: A Place and Space

As children need your time and your interest and their own independent time to grow through creative endeavors, they need space— both physical space and mental space.

The physical space does not have to be large, but try to let them have some kind of table to work on, or a corner of a room in which to set up the farmyard they are putting together or the scrapbook they are making. The table can be as simple as one you buy at a garage sale, but it is a rich investment if they know that it is their table, one on which they can keep their things. They see your space for your activities—the kitchen cabinet, the worktable, your table for art work, or the workbench—and they know they have a similar place of their own for individual (or joint) pursuits.

Give them space and a place for their own possessions, a special shelf, a drawer, or section of cupboard; a place in which they can keep things precious to them—the colored rocks that look like jewels; the design made with hammer, nails, and scrap lumber, the scraps of fabric for doll clothes. . . . The sense of independence, the feeling of "this is all mine," the defining of each one's own territory are important to keeping children wanting to move ahead. If children share a room, each can still have a sense of privacy in his or her own area. Create a divider from shelves or use a furniture arrangement to give a feeling of separateness, to let each know that "this part of the room is mine."

Don't demand of yourself or of them an immaculate room free from all that is useless in your eyes. Neatness and order help, but a constant stress on this can overwhelm children.

If space is at a minimum, you can attach a pegboard with hooks on the back of a door or construct a pegboard wall, one section for each child's own use. You can use inexpensive cardboard storage boxes or plastic tubs that fit under the beds as storage spaces for their own belongings. *Label these boxes with their own names with a marking pen—they will like the feeling of identity this gives.* Colorful tubs marked with their own names can be placed on shelves that they can share with another brother or sister. These tubs help keep toys separate and eliminate a hodge-podge that can clutter a child's thinking.

In guiding your children's play and in choosing toys, be conscious of how easily sex-role patterns can be formed. If you forbid your boy to play with a cooking set, or if your daughter shows a strong interest in trucks or machinery, and if you make fun of this interest and she is offered play things you consider "for girls only," sex-role stereotyping can easily occur. Ask yourself, "Do I really want my child to have the values I am reflecting? What attitudes toward sex roles do I want to transmit to my child?"

From Us—For Them: Things to Work With

Just as toys do not have to be purchased to be beneficial, materials for creative expression are all around. Paper for scrapbooks can be cut from paper sacks. Finger paints can be made from food coloring and liquid starch. Play dough for modeling can be made from equal parts of flour and salt with enough water added to make a stiff dough, and food coloring added for a special tint.

Have a special place in your home for a surprise box. Put in this box colored fabric, yarn, buttons, margarine tubs, string, old magazines, paper plates, and other interesting odds and ends. Let your children create whatever they wish from this. You can first show them an example of various possibilities: a collage from old magazine pictures, perhaps, or a yarn or a string design pasted on colored paper. Then let them feel free to explore their imagination with the contents of the box.

Let them see your own imaginative endeavors—taking what is to what might be possible, and they can catch the same spirit.

Keeping an imaginative eye on the things you discard can help you (and your children) see how they can be used to make something else. And the resulting blend of ecology, economy, and imagination can be adopted by your children to help them realize new discoveries.

The following list gives just a sample of the possibilities that abound.

- Old flashlight—toy X-ray device
- Oatmeal boxes—drums, stacking toys, building blocks
- Discarded window shades—surface to paint on
- Plastic tops from coffee containers, etc.— clock faces
- Egg cartons—jewelry boxes (They can be painted gold or silver.)
- Colored toothpicks—to make lines, shapes, and designs
- Old newspapers—paper-mache
- Margarine containers—containers for finger paints and water colors
- Empty television cabinet—puppet stage
- Paper bags—hand puppets
- Pieces of yarn, lace, string, cotton— "brushes" for pictures they can feel
- Snap clothes pins and pieces of foam rubber—paint "brushes"

These are ordinary uses for ordinary materials. What other uses of left-over materials can you think of?

_____

_____

_____

At this time, it is good to again point out what was stressed earlier: *Stimulate, don't stifle.* For beneficial as all of this is, beneficial as play is, giving children *too much* to absorb allows them little mental space to fully benefit from any one experience. A mother of three pre-kindergarten children recognized this as she complained: "Our children have innumerable toys. The grandparents shower toys upon them. They are all over the house, all over their room, every place."

As she continued to describe her children's play, I could see that these children were really overstimulated. These children were really smothered with toys, few of them really enriching the children. Their very number virtually wiped out their good. Because space was at a premium in this home, I suggested that the toys be stored in under-the-bed boxes or large plastic containers in the basement, then alternated in use, so that each toy could serve to benefit the child. This was definitely a case where "more is less."

Just as one mother found too many toys one grand confusion, another parent realized the opposite effect by limiting the number of toys to be enjoyed at one time, by alternating their use.

A plastic wagon filled with plastic blocks could entertain Todd (at eight months) for a half an hour or longer. When he was two, a pull toy with a removable driver could keep him engrossed for an hour. When he played with this toy, he kept talking aloud about the toy figure, and imaginatively continued to construct other pictures in his mind as he was caught up in play and in learning. He would talk about the wooden pilot of the toy plane going to Chicago, talk about his dad going to Chicago, live a variety of experiences with just one toy.

This child had many more toys available to him, but they were not all available at one time. They were alternated in use. The boy's mother said, "One thing I tried to do was not give Todd too many toys at one time." Todd, completely delighted, would draw out of only one toy, and out of himself, imaginative enrichment. He was truly absorbing the toy completely, and he exemplified the first element of creativity, a real observation and awareness. This intense observation evolved to reflect other creative resources including imagination, curiosity, independence, freedom to fail, and further awareness.

ADDED ACTIVITIES TO HELP DEVELOP A CHILD'S INNER RESOURCES

By now you should have a picture of what you can give in the way of materials and what you can give of yourself to develop creative thinking and its resultant inner resources. You have seen that interest and attention, time for your child, place and space, and things to work/play/create with—all are needed. And you have focused on some activities helpful to this development, but there are added creative activities which should be considered.

Puppets and Play Acting

Playing with puppets is an activity which is especially beneficial in developing inner supports:

Two-year-old Joseph took his puppet, Ernie, everywhere. He slept with Ernie; he talked to him; he scolded Ernie for his own errors; he treated the puppet as a companion, and took him along when the family went out to eat. Joseph took on the character of the puppet and alternated in playing different roles with him.

When he was three, Joseph tried to cheer up a saddened family member by saying, "You be big Ernie. I be little Ernie. We talk to each other." Joseph was learning independence, imagination, solving problems, expressing feelings, trying out different roles—and benefiting from puppet play in many ways.

To be helpful, puppets do not have to be expensive; they can easily be made from materials around the home. A two-year-old can be delighted with a Red Riding Hood puppet (or one of a favorite nursery rhyme or fairy tale character) made from something as simple as a flat stick used as a base on which a cut-out figure is attached. You can make an entire set of storybook characters this way. Paste the appropriate clothing on the figures, and use them to help your child act out the stories. Puppets made from stockings (with a face drawn on the foot of the stocking) can be made quickly and are easy to manipulate. A paper sack with a face drawn on it and holes cut out of the sides for fingers (for the puppet arms) is another very simple device which can provide a child with much imaginative play.

Similarly, imaginative play, in which a child takes on the character of another in play acting helps forge inner development. In such play a child learns to receive appreciation from others, to share with various ages of children (or adults), to develop confidence, to try out different experiences through playing different roles, including those of the adult world. Play acting can be as simple as the two-year-old repeatedly wanting to change roles and saying, "You be Marie. I'll be Aunt Grace. I come to visit you." Or, it can be much more complicated and shared with various ages of children who present an actual play for a group of approving parents.

Making Things: Taking "What Is" to "What Might Be Possible"

Self-esteem can be fostered with all forms of creative expression, and often this expression takes the form of making things, of creating something out of something else. As we have seen, in creating something, in bringing a new product into being, children put their stamp of themselves on something outside of themselves. They experience added feelings of achievement as they see this product of themselves.

Their (and your) imagination can produce repeated delights—can be the base for learning to come up with new decisions, for dealing with change, for hope, for relying upon themselves for answers, for seeing familiar things in a new light. It can help them be glad to be in a world that does not become old to them but keeps furnishing materials for new insights.

Making things can give a wealth of satisfaction. The next section contains suggestions which can stimulate ideas of your own. Check the suggestions you wish to adopt and add any ideas of your own that you wish to share with your child.

Making things can build children's self-esteem:

- Pieces of lace, yarn, cotton, string, wire, seeds, pieces of bark, fabric, artificial leaves, construction paper, cardboard, old shingles, buttons, or weathered wood, etc., can help children make a picture to feel. Choose a simple design for the two-to-three year olds; a more complicated design for the four-to-five year olds. After showing them your picture, let them design a picture of their own. This picture can illustrate a favorite song, a character, or a place from a favorite book, or simply how they feel. You can work alongside of them. Select materials and arrange them on a cardboard base, old shingle, or wood, and they can watch and get ideas of their own while you paste your pictures on the base. Talk about the different textures you use.

• With clay and dried plants, small shells, and colored rocks show them how you make a "space picture." Arrange small, dried plants for trees in a clay base: set this in a sea shell or flat container. Clay can be covered with colored rocks or small shells.

• From old magazines, wrapping paper or paper sacks, paste, crayons or marking pens, help them cut out pictures to paste (or stick on using double-stick tape) on wrapping paper pages which have been stapled or sewn together to form a book. You can give your children a title for each book, and they can illustrate it with pictures they find. Titles can focus on your children to add to their sense of identity, titles such as, "Things I Like to Eat," or "Friends I Would Like to Have," or simply, "Me." If they tell you a story about their pictures write their story below the corresponding pictures.

They can draw or paint their own experiences and tell you about them. They can punch holes in the paper and lace it together, or they can staple it together to make a book. They can fill the book with various designs of their own made from the different colors of paper; they can tell you about their drawings or designs, and you can write their story for them.

- With hammer, nails, wood, glue, and *guidance* let them build whatever they wish or simply pound in a design of their own on the boards. To help them know the initials of their name, you can outline these with clearly visible dots with a marking pen, and they can "write" their name with the nails.

- With 12-by-18-inch sheets of construction paper and washable marking pens, water-color crayons, or crayons; or with yarn, needle and children's scissors, outline your children's names or initials with dots on the paper. They can follow the dots with the marking pens or crayons to form their individual names, or they can use the yarn to outline their initials. The paper can be fringed with a blunt scissors and used as their individual placemats.

- With pieces of plain fabric and crayons, they can draw their own designs on the fabric, fringe the edges, and make a wall hanging for their rooms.

These few ideas of making things, of seeing the visible expression of creativity, can be added to as imagination continues. Ask your children for ideas of their own. (A three-year-old child, for instance, might find possibilities for margarine tubs or film cans you would not have thought of.) Give *them* the delight of helping *you* learn.

Other Art Materials

Give your children finger paints, clay, crayons, watercolor crayons, paper and other materials with which they can express themselves. Cover a work space with a heavy piece of plastic; give them water colors, paper, and a brush to use, or let them use finger paints and see how colors blend under their own hands. Pent-up emotions can be released through such activities. Let them express themselves. Don't feel it is necessary to tell them *what* to do or what to express, but, if you wish, you can suggest they:

- Show the way they feel when they are angry, sad, happy, afraid. (Show the way they feel when they hear wind in the tree outside the window, when it storms or rains, or when they see lightning flash in the sky.) This helps show them you respect their feelings. Let them tell you about their work and their feelings.

- Show what they would like to be when they grow up.

These, of course, are just a few ideas to stimulate your own imagination about the creative growth of your children. If you wish, you can write what they tell you about their creation on a special card and place both their work and their words where they can easily be seen or in a special Family Display area. You can help your children feel good about themselves when they see that *you value what they have produced* and when they see the expression of themselves displayed for others.

Fill a Child's Mind With
Creative Experiences and Learning

Again, we stress—as you help your children reach to the wonder of the world about them, talk often to them about their experiences. It is not just to become aware of experiences, but to make new associations from them. You can help them see these associations. During a walk in the woods on an autumn day, they can hear the leaves crackle under their feet, collect colored leaves to place in a vase in their rooms, see the birds scatter from a tree to fly south for the winter. Their minds can be filled with a wealth of new experiences and new associations.

With a variety of words and new associations, your children can continue to think and reach out and wonder and make new associations. You can ask questions such as, "What do those bare branches remind you of?" "What colors do you see in the gravel on the path?" "Do you think the leaf could sail in the water in the sink? Let's take it home and try to find out."

Share imagery and ideas with them such as, "The smoke is like a dirty finger rubbing across the sky," or "Let's collect these autumn weeds to take home and make a bouquet."

Thoughts grow from thoughts, and vocabulary grows with words and associations that develop from creative experiences. The next section will focus more directly on building the use of language, but so much of children's language development is associated with creative experience that mention must also be made of this here. Simple creative experiences can help fill a child's mind with new associations. The diagram on page 144 shows this.

In the spaces in the diagram, list creative activities your children might experience. Then think of the associations they might have from these experiences and the learning that results. Fill in "the child's mind" with these new associations, following the example shown in the diagram.

New Associations:

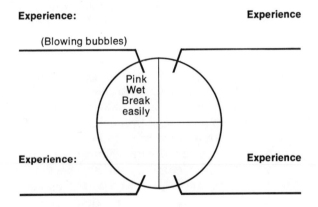

Experience:

(Blowing bubbles)

Pink
Wet
Break
easily

Experience

Experience:

Experience

In an activity as simple as blowing bubbles, for instance, your children might see the different colors, might realize they break easily, that they can make different shapes, etc. They are *aware* that they are colorful, wet, and break easily. They *observe* this, and this can lead them to *wonder why* they are colorful and why they break so easily. *Curious,* they can feel imaginative and *free* and *independent* enough to try to blow bubbles that won't break immediately or that have a different color or

144

size or shape. They can evaluate and judge and realize that they can, to some extent, control their size, can break the bubbles or, if careful, can let them rest on their hands. They have now experienced and learned a variety of new information. They perhaps can also observe that the bubbles are the colors of objects familiar to them, that they can be made in various shapes similar to shapes of things with which they are already familiar.

It is exciting to see how your children's experiences can result in new learning, to see how easily you can help fill your child's mind. As you continue to be with your children, you can continue to enrich their minds—by giving them your time and interest, a place and space in which to work. As you give them materials to work with—as you give clay to a three-year-old, perhaps, and he learns it is soft, squishy, movable, and that he can make it into something, or, as you first give a two-year-old crayons or finger paints and blank paper, and she learns she herself can control the colors, that *she* is causing those funny, squiggly lines to appear, that she is causing change—as you do this, you are also causing change; you are helping your children to learn.

COMMUNICATION AND CREATIVITY

"When I make something, I want to show it to someone," a parent said recently. "I want to share what I have created."

A young friend agreed, "I just learned cake decorating. I am so proud of my work. I have a real sense of achievement. I feel good about what I have done. I want to show it to my husband."

Another said, "I always felt especially creative in sewing and designing clothes for my daughter. I felt very good about myself when I was finished. I couldn't wait to show someone what I had done. I wanted to share. It wasn't just the wanting to show what I had done, but in some way to share the experience I felt."

When we create something, we feel good about ourselves. Whether it is concocting a new recipe or designing a new room—or a new bridge, or plan for the backyard garage, the process and the product enriches us. And we want to share that enrichment.

Children, in creating, also want to share. When a two-year-old boy excitedly points to a pair of upright candles on the table, and says, "Look . . . an H!" he wants to share what is happening inside of him. When a five-year-old girl colors a rainbow of designs on sheets of purple and pink and yellow note pad paper, and then staples them together and gives you this book she has made just for you, she wants to share both product and what she feels inside. In such sharing, children offer the gifts of themselves.

This is why it is especially important to be available to your children, to really listen to what they are saying, to help them recapture the excitement in what they have done, to show them with what you say and how you listen that you are ready to enter their world and to feel with them their pleasure. The sharing adds to the enlargement of both you and your children. Together you have grown with the new experience.

Sometimes creation brings with it doubts and inner questioning as to how what we have created will be received. It is as if something inside of us is pushing us to express ourselves, and yet we are not sure what others will think of our expression. Sometimes, such inner doubt in children occurs because they begin to compare themselves in the light of others.

Five-year-old Jan was such a child: "I don't like this house I drew," she stated as she began to draw house after house. "My houses don't look like Maggie's houses." Even if her friend, Maggie, was not present, Jan had a clear picture of her friend's house. She had already placed her own criteria of acceptance on her work. Her inner acceptance of self in her work could not be reached at that time unless it in some way measured up to those criteria she had placed on herself. But, interestingly, she continued to draw houses. Her doubt did not cause her to give up. Something was urging her inside to continue.

An hour later, she began another activity. She joined two adult friends who, with watercolor crayons, were drawing pictures on write-on slides to be used for an at-home slide show. Jan very freely expressed herself on each slide, not wanting to imitate in any way what her adult friends had done. She was very much herself in her

drawings, eager to see her slides
placed in the projector and watch the
resulting slide show, excited to see her
contribution to the whole project, and
happy with herself.

The slide show was entirely new activity for
her. She had not experienced this before, and
neither had any of her small friends (who were
not present). There were no standards against
which she was measuring herself. It was a
sharp lesson on the fragility of a child's inner
sense of self, what influences it, and how it is
molded.

It was also a lesson on how communication
can be a positive reinforcing, or healing, agent
to a sense of self. As children express themselves in such creative endeavors, you can
show them an added acceptance of self as you
accept what they have made, as they finally
accept within themselves the fact that you do
not expect their work to be like that of anyone
else, that if it were, it really would not express
their ownselves, that their work has merit
because it is theirs alone, not because it is a
reflection of someone else's vision.

STIFLING CREATIVITY OR
KEEPING IT ALIVE

In Section II you saw how important it is to
listen and talk to your children in order that
you might better fill their needs, how communication affects children's self-image. How
you listen or do not listen to your children,
what you say or do not say to them, the
encouraging or discouraging statements you

make can either stifle creativity and learning or push it forward.

The following dialogues show various ways talk can discourage creativity. Following each example, write an opposite statement that would encourage creativity.

Child: Look at the pretty shapes the snow-flakes make on the window!
Parent: (sharply) I can't now. I'm too busy!

Your response: _____

_____

_____

Child: (Rushing in from school) Look what I brought you—all these pretty leaves. Look, they're red, yellow . . . but some are brown. What makes the leaves turn brown? Can you put these in a vase? Can I save them?
Mother: You ask too many questions. Look those leaves are crumbling all over my clean floor after I just got everything cleaned up for the party tonight!

Your response: _____

_____

_____

Son: Dad, how come you never use that paper holder I made for you for your birthday, the one Aunt Judy helped me with?
Father: Paper holder? I can't seem to remember . . . Oh yes, that thing you

brought home the other month made from a clothespin and some wood. Let's see—where did I put it?

Your response: _____

_____

_____

Mother: Look at the junk you have in your room! What's this bent coat hanger for? Why are you saving that in your desk? And what is the mirror frame without a mirror in it left there for? What in the world are you doing with these things? You're old enough to straighten your room!

Child: Can't you see . . . I've made a duck out of that coat hanger. Please let me keep it. And I use that mirror frame to draw squares around. We're learning about squares, circles, and triangles in school. See all the squares I've made.

Mother: What an imagination you've got! You'd be a lot better off without it. At least you'd have a neater room!

Your response: _____

_____

_____

Child: Jenny says her mother always lets her make Christmas tree ornaments for the tree. Why can't I make some? I heard this recipe on *Magic, Magic, Everywhere* on TV. But I forgot it. But the lady said all you have to do is call

150

the station, and they'll mail you the directions. Can't I do this? I think all you need is flour and water and . . . .

Mother: You know, I want our tree to look perfect. You just wait till you're older, and then maybe you can help. Anyway, what would those decorations look like with the red velvet roses and gold fans I'm going to use this year? You know how everyone likes my trees—says they are really unusual. It's not that I don't want you to help, but just wait until you can do things better.

Your response: _____

_____

_____

Unusual answers to give children? Not really. Listening to yourself can tell you this. Sometimes, we all fail to listen to our own responses to our children, listening to see just how our communication, verbal and non-verbal, reflects on stifled creativity. It is not that you should drop everything at the whim of your children. You have needs too. And you can state your needs and feelings to your children so they can understand what is going on within you. Obviously, it is not that you do not want to be bothered with your children; it is just that often you may not state your needs properly to them.

In the first example, for instance, just watching the tone of voice and adding, perhaps, even such a simple statement as, "In ten minutes I'll be there, and I can really see them better when I have more time," could change the effect considerably.

Or, in the example with the leaves, the mother could simply say, "I've got everything cleaned up for the party. Let's put these leaves in a box for now; and tomorrow, when I have more time, I'll find a vase, and we can put them in your room."

Ask yourself, "What comments do I make which might stifle creativity?" If they resemble the ones just examined, practice in changing discouraging to encouraging responses as in the next exercise can help you see how communication affects creativity.

Discourage Creativity	Encourage Creativity
Do as I say. Use these colors.	
You might make a mistake.	
A tree! That doesn't look like a tree to me.	
Here, let me make that. You take too long.	

Statements such as the following can change the negative effects and foster continued creative motivation:

- I like the purple, pink and yellow you used.
- I'm glad you're going to try.

152

- That's an interesting tree—a black tree— tell me about your tree.
- Don't worry. A lot of new things I try take me a long time.

Knowing about the possible need to change your ways can give you a start in being different the next time around.

To Develop Creativity: Should Do—Should Not Do

Here is a check-list you can use of things *you should do* and things *you should not do* to keep creativity alive in your children. Read over this list, and keep it in mind. You may want to check the "Do's" you think would be particularly helpful for your child, and you can also check those "Don't's" that you feel represent things that you want to correct.

Do's

- If you like something they make, tell them you like it. _____
- Allow children to attempt things on their own. _____
- Ask children to *tell* you about their work. Don't say, "What is that?" _____

Don't's

- Scold if they make a mess in a creative project. Plan for this ahead of time by giving them a space where making a mess doesn't matter. _____
- Expect perfection. _____

- Suggest that your children should make something exactly as you did, so they will learn correctly. ____
- Allow only a short, set period of time for a creative project. ____
- Question your children about everything on which they are working. ____
- Constantly suggest changes which will improve their project. ____
- Fill the day so full that children have no time of their own. ____

Suggesting that your children's work resemble yours, limiting their time, laughing at odd-looking drawings, and expecting perfection can stifle creativity. And even if you are interested in your children's work, don't smother their growth by being overly present. Constantly questioning your children about their projects, always suggesting changes which will improve their work, stimulating them with too many activities are all ways of dispensing harmful medicine to the creative process. They can cripple it or cause it to wither and die.

One does not keep creativity alive by insisting that all trees look alike or by placing adult dimensions on a child's creative attempts. You help when you allow your children to be free enough to express their own being, when you listen to what they have to tell you about their work, when you do not expect perfection, and when keeping a perfectly neat home does not take higher priority than the creative growth of your child.

Do You Agree or Do You Disagree?

Here is an activity you can do alone if you wish to examine your own thinking about creativity and its role in developing inner growth in children. Read each statement, then circle either A (agree) or D (disagree) accordingly. If you wish, you can modify any statement in order to agree with it. This activity is also good to share with a partner or in a group. In these latter cases, you can proceed in the same manner, changing the wording in any statement so that you can come to an agreement. If you cannot agree even when the words are changed, agree to disagree. Do not be concerned with "right" or "wrong" statements as such—only how you feel about each statement.

A D **1.** When a child is in a preschool program, it is the role of the school to further creativity in the child.

A D **2.** The creative child is an artistic child.

A D **3.** Development of the senses comes naturally to the child.

A D **4.** It is equally important for a child to have an immaculate, neat room with nothing out of place as it is to have a room in which he or she saves "interesting things," or "junk" as some might call it.

A D **5.** All children are creative.

A D **6.** The process, the actual doing, in creativity can be a purely mental activity.

A D **7.** The process in creativity, what happens inside children as they are creating, is more important than the product (what is created).

A D **8.** A nonimaginative parent cannot help a child develop creative expression.

A D **9.** A child who paints a picture which you understand is more creative than a child who paints something you do not understand.

A D **10.** A child can learn without being in any way creative.

These statements can help you continue to think about your importance in nurturing the creative expressions of your young children. As they move from their first days of infancy to interact more and more with people and objects external to themselves—to the group play of the three-year-olds—to the highly imaginative stage of the four- or five-year-olds able to develop abstract thinking—your children create their own being. Keep remembering—for now you are the prime forces in the world with which they interact and from which they are drawing creative nourishment.

CHANGE-GROWTH

To see how you have changed as you have worked through these pages on creativity, go back to the self-inventory at the beginning of this section. Leave your original responses, but add any present change directly above your original response. Compare your changed responses. In what way have you changed? List these changes below.

_____

_____

_____

_____

You now see more clearly that creativity can add to self-esteem, to the ability to adapt to change, to an exhilaration of oneself in realizing, "I have within me the power to change something." As you see this, you, too can experience the exhilaration of feeling, "I, too, am changed."

The following resolution can help you stay aware of your own creative role in your children's continual "becoming themselves." As you read this, underline those parts especially important to you. Try to keep them in mind. They can be the basis for your own individual goal in these never to be repeated first days of helping your child—for life.

Resolved, as a Parent, I Will . . .

As a parent, I realize that I am a vital creative factor in *my children's* creative experiences as they, individually, discover themselves. I realize that they first must know themselves as they interact with the world before they understand others. I realize that much of what I do can lead them to this knowledge.

And so, I will continually try to develop a balanced climate for creative growth: of affection, understanding, acceptance, freedom, and control. In this climate I will take time to help my children develop an awareness of the world and its renewed wonder. I will take time to encourage my children to learn about their world to help them develop the components of creativity—awareness and observation, curiosity, imagination, freedom, independence, and the freedom to fail. I will try to remember that these components are also steps to learning. And I will try to remember that my actions can foster or stifle my children's natural urge to create.

I will take time to stimulate and also take care not to smother—knowing that children need mental space as well as physical space for continual discovery in their process of "becoming."

I will take time to help them see new possibilities in familiar objects of everyday living. I will take time to offer them new experiences which can join together to give birth to new learning, realizing that in this discovery they are continuing to "re-create" themselves.

I will try to realize that in doing these things I am helping them develop inner resources vital to their future, that I am helping develop in them a base for hope, for coping in a changing world, a base for continuing to bring "the new" into life.

section 4

Language, Learning, and Living

We can never be born enough. We are human beings; for whom birth is a supremely welcome mystery, the mystery of of growing . . .
—E. E. Cummings

"He's p'obably thinkin' . . . thinkin' about his friends," the two-year-old says about the lightning bug held in cupped hands.

"I happy with myself . . . I happy with you . . . You happy with you? . . . I happy with us," the child says, and tells us that all is right with his world.

Children's language is spontaneously creative as they bring their thoughts to life. As they fashion aloud their individual feelings, they are truly bringing "the new" to the world. In this process, they experience one of the most satisfying of all creative ventures.

The process starts with their very first words. From sounds and syllables, children bring to life words and the power of their use. They not only create something new, something that is *apart* from themselves, but they create something that at the same time becomes *a part* of themselves. With language, they change their very being; they add a new way to comprehend the world they are discovering.

Think about it, this mystifying process . . . of sounds . . . words . . . language. It visibly begins when, from the prenatal cushioning of quiet, infants are thrust into a world vibrant with movement and stimulation. Sense stimulations are fairly bursting around them. As infants, they feel the comfort of being held. They hear the tones of caring voices. Progressively, they focus on a multitude of objects and the presence of people. Inside of them, they feel the urge to grow. From an existence of quiet, they are suddenly involved with touching, tasting, smelling, seeing, and hearing. And they are involved in hearing themselves.

As children hear sounds around them, they themselves make sounds. The sounds mix with the other sensory impressions they experience and with their push to grow and reach out as they begin to form their identity, to learn about, and to have some control over the new world. The sounds do not stand in isolation. They couple with continuing sense impressions in an environment that adds meaning to sounds. And language develops.

From prenatal silence to a child of six with a vocabulary of thousands upon thousands of words, from your infant's first cry to a kindergarten child using language to formulate ideas, to express thoughts and feelings, to see cause and effect, to talk to others as he or she shares meanings with others—how does this all come about?

In examining this transformation, this very literal "crossing over" from the world of quiet to the almost awesome world of verbal communication, we will:

- Look more closely at the general development of language;
- Study its importance to the life of the child;
- Look more thoroughly at the "ingredients" parents can give to help develop language according to various stages of growth;
- Examine suggestions for developing language during the infant-to-six years. These suggestions will include ideas for the following:
  - Games and activities that help develop language

- Developing meaning of words
- Helping your child become aware of printed words
- Helping language come to life
- Television, language, and thought.

THE GENERAL DEVELOPMENT OF LANGUAGE

The development of children's language is shaped by sensory stimulations combined with the parent's response and the particular environment they provide for them. Whether this development is sluggish or alive depends a great deal on the type of human interaction between children and you who care for them.

As background to the examination of language development, keep in mind that:

- Language flourishes in a climate which allows for safe exploration, one which offers a variety of sensory stimuli and which fosters steps to creative growth: awareness, observation, curiosity, imagination, and the freedom to fail.

- Talking to your children, from infancy on, is vital to language development.

- The development of language adds to a child's accomplishments. As children continue to feel good about themselves, as they are allowed a climate of creative exploration offering a variety of stimulation and a freedom to move and explore, they continue to feel free to reach out to learn, to try new things, to "become themselves." Trying out more language is part of this continuous cycle of development. It is part of their overall push to grow and to learn.

- A climate that fosters self-esteem and creative exploration is a climate in which spontaneous talk can easily occur between parent and child. Your responses are vital to the development of your child's ability with language.

Take time now to stop and reflect on your role in developing your child's language. The self-inventory below can help you see a reflection of yourself.

A LANGUAGE SELF-INVENTORY

1. How would you define language? _____

    _____

    _____

    _____

2. Why do you want your child to possess language skills?_____

    _____

    _____

    _____

3. Rank yourself according to your capability to help develop your child's language: Circle the appropriate number:

    Very capable   Capable   Not capable
        5   4   3   2   1

4. Explain the reason for your choice: ___

    _____

    _____

    _____

5. What is required of you to help develop language in your child? _____

   _____

   _____

   _____

6. What strengths do you possess which can help develop your child's language skills? (Patience, interest, attention, etc.)

   _____

   _____

   _____

7. What weaknesses do you have which might hamper language development?

   _____

   _____

   _____

8. Do you think that the amount of formal education a parent possesses *necessarily* influences the child's language development? _____

   _____

   _____

   _____

9. Do you think a nonworking mother is *necessarily* a better influence on the child's language development than a working mother? _____

   _____

   _____

10. What factors do you think are most influential in raising a competent child who possesses adequate language skills?

_____

_____

_____

11. How does a parent's language affect a child's self-worth and creative expression? _____

_____

_____

_____

12. What has this (self-worth and creative expression) to do with a child's use of language? _____

_____

_____

_____

13. List five specific sensory or creative experiences which could be the base for developing your child's language. _____

_____

_____

_____

14. List five things you are now doing which help develop your child's language. _____

_____

_____

An inventory is stock-taking time. How is your "stock" already on hand? Working through the preceding sections on self-esteem and creativity should help you feel more "supplied" in nurturing your child's language development. You should feel more positive about your strengths in helping your child. And as for self-worth and creative experiences—you have already seen the influence they have on your child's use of language.

The link between fostering a child's creative expression and developing language is a strong one, and almost anything you have done toward nurturing creativity will build language skill. Similarly, anything you have done to help develop a true self-esteem will help your child use language.

So, you can feel that you are already well on the way to giving your child a good start toward using words. Continue to build upon this feeling; and, don't feel any less competent because you work away from home some of the day, or because you are a single parent, or because you might not possess a high school diploma. These things are not necessarily measures of the kind of help your child needs.

By now, you should see that your responses do not have to be planned-out activities—that your strengths as a parent and competency in your child can go along with everyday living. Your role in developing language is a vital role, but a far from frightening one. Exciting, challenging, creative, for-life—these more aptly describe your days as you continue to follow your child in the main steps toward language development.

STEPS IN
LANGUAGE DEVELOPMENT

Steps in language development are listed below. Read them carefully; then underline the step which indicates the language stage of your child.

1. Comes from a world of prenatal quiet of the womb.
2. Enters a world of sense stimulation. Lights, colors, noises, touching, tasting, smelling, seeing, hearing are continually experienced. Sounds are a vibrant part of this sensory stimuli.
3. Hears sounds and sorts them out. Human voices are part of the sounds. Some sounds are heard more than others. Some sounds mean more than others. (A mother's voice, for instance, couples with the warmth of her body as she holds, feeds, and talks to her child.)
4. Hears sounds and tries out own sounds. Cries, gurgles, coos, babbles, etc. Usually the sounds of p-b-m-n come first. Then t-g-d-k, and lastly l-b-r-and s.
5. Learns to sort out sounds. Can distinguish sounds of footsteps, voices, and the like.
6. Begins to imitate sounds and discards those which are not heard. Certain syllables *sound* like those he or she hears. More and more a child is receptive to language and increasingly uses syllables that he or she hears other people use.
7. Comes to realize that sounds identify familiar things. By repeating and responding encouragingly to syllables that sound like

words, parents and those close to the child can help him or her identify sounds with objects and people. The word-label is born; the child makes words.

8. Adds associative meanings of words. From reactions of parents and others, from tones in voices and from nonverbal cues, from the environment in which words are heard, the child develops the meaning of words.

9. Language continues to develop: from single words to two-word statements to individually created sentences, to an increasingly adequate and clear *use* of language. In an environment which provides safe exploration and encouraging response to activities, language develops.

The chart on the next page shows these steps involved in language development. Study this chart, and, if you wish, write in examples of your own child's experiences.

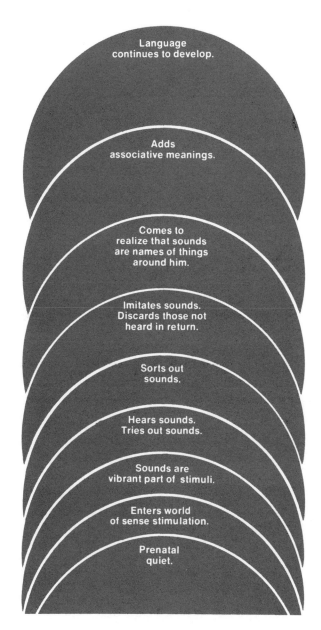

Language continues to develop.

Adds associative meanings.

Comes to realize that sounds are names of things around him.

Imitates sounds. Discards those not heard in return.

Sorts out sounds.

Hears sounds. Tries out sounds.

Sounds are vibrant part of stimuli.

Enters world of sense stimulation.

Prenatal quiet.

171

THE IMPORTANCE OF LANGUAGE

Myriad accomplishments bring a child from infancy to the magic of the "talking world." Each of the child's accomplishments brings new pleasure to the parents. There is the first smile, the first patty-cake, the first waving goodbye, the crawling and sitting alone and handling of the spoon and drinking from a cup . . . .

And then, there comes the day when that excitement is different—deeper. It is the day when these first sounds are put together in what seems to you is your child's first word. You call it that—those first meaningful sounds. And whenever they are repeated, you respond appropriately. If they sound like "mama," or "da-da," you appear or in some way show encouraging response. They become words through your responses.

It does not take long to learn that your infant is a great imitator of sounds. You saw this imitation earlier—how he or she learned the baby games. Now, you see how words and even short sentences are copied. The word "goggie" for "doggie" is added, perhaps, and you might hear "Wo goggie go?" repeated back to you from the first "Where did doggie go?" question you repeatedly asked your one-year-old.

Years later the remembrance of your infant's first talk can still stir you, for the pleasure you feel over the first words is different from the pleasure that you felt over the earlier accomplishments. This is not just another childhood development to be recorded in a baby book. You recognize that language is special development. It links your child to his or her world in a totally new way. With language, your child possesses a distinguishing mark of being human.

As you see your children's speech continue to develop, you can see that language gives them a vital inner resource. They can now begin to participate in and manage their world in yet another fashion—different from those earlier achievements when they began to crawl and pull themselves up. As they begin to call out "da-da," and daddy appears, or "ma-ma" and mama comes, as they begin to tell you their needs and feelings, they experience a new control over their environment. You watch this mastery of language and environment begin on a small scale, then spread as they begin to identify, and thus further interact, with the people and things about them.

The infant's words do not, of course, develop spontaneously. This special human quality of speech develops, with the interaction of a variety of sense stimulations, as he or she is given a chance for free exploration in which movement (motor skills) can bring further sense stimulations. And, it must be stressed, it develops through contact with people who *care and respond.*

Words and language patterns begin to be developed long before the first word is actually heard. The first smiles, cries, laughs, babbling, patty-cakes, and kisses are first attempts at communication. How you respond to these attempts and *to all activities* are powerful influences to speech. Your influence begins when you first hold your child in your arms.

What Is Language?

So vital is human love, attention, and response to language development, that infants who are isolated from this show a halting pattern of language development. This is very understandable when we consider what language really is. Language is not just syllables strung together. It is not just symbols or words that represent things. It is not just the rules of putting these symbols together or not just a sound or sounds that label a thing or a person.

Language is all of this *coupled with all of the inside reactions that arise when one hears a word being spoken.* Language is words, symbols, sounds, and signs, of course, but, is also the meanings and reactions to words felt inside of the person. And you, who are closest to your child in these early years, help give these meanings.

Language enables your child to share his or her particular meaning with someone else. Language helps keep one human from standing in isolation from another.

In this interaction, *your talk* draws out *your child's talk.* Your words are spontaneous as you go about the many tasks of childcare. But your words of "I love you," and "let me rock you awhile," and all of the other things you say blend with the tones you use, and your touch, and the look in your eyes that convey to even a very young child the first faint stirrings of meanings of words.

Meanings of Words

And so, words and meaning develop. From your day-to-day use from within you, words and meaning continue to settle within your child. As your baby is held in your arms, or plays at your feet, crawls, stands, takes your hand and tries out the first faltering steps, as you play together on the lawn, and as you share the first days of school, the way you talk is a powerful influence on the way your child

will talk. What you say and the way you respond couples with inner experiences your child feels to help give language. *From the beginning, you have stirred words and meanings into the essence of your child's life.*

In this manner, you give your child words. And you give much more. You give language—with the associative meanings of words, meaning that can come back in a flash decades later. As the years go on, these early meanings will be added to and modified. But the memories of words learned in childhood do leap back into a later adult presence. Those meanings you help implant in your child can suddenly reappear decades later . . . .

You know how it is with words—how they flash back across the years to bring with them pictures of memories pushed way back in the crevices of your childhood. Maybe it is the word, "picnic." It might come back to you when you hear the word or walk through the park where you had your first picnic. The games, the laughter, the taste of hot dogs and roasted marshmallows, all come back in a rush. They last a long time—the pictures (and meanings), early words stamp our being.

What words do you remember that have meanings associated to your childhood? What pictures of now do you hope your child will keep in his album of himself?

I remember:_____

_____

I hope my child will remember:_____

_____

_____

WHAT CAN A PARENT GIVE
TO HELP DEVELOP LANGUAGE?

What ingredients can you give that are necessary for learning and using language? An opportunity for sensory stimulation, a chance for safe exploration that allows for body movement (both small and large movement), and loving response in both verbal and nonverbal ways—it's a checklist to mentally keep before you as you find the excitement in helping your children grow.

To gain a better understanding of how these factors work with one another in the child's total environment, let us look at them separately in the various stages from infancy to six years of age. This does not mean there are set guidelines for each stage of language development. We are looking at these separate stages only to see, in a general way, how language develops. Normal children do not, of course, fit into such exact outlines. They have very individual developments.

The examples below indicate children's language needs and how they can be met at various ages. Many of these examples are also helpful in growth stages other than the specific stage listed. Do not think that these are the only examples you can follow. They are *only suggestions* for types of activities. (There is space provided for you to write in additional activities that you think would be helpful. And of course it is not necessary to follow each suggestion. This could be an overwhelming task and could really detract from your sincere care for your child. In other words, don't overdo your concern. Children can absorb your feeling of stress.

FROM INFANT TO TODDLER

One-to-Six-Months

Sensory stimulation: Provide colorful mobiles, musical toys to roll or push, colorful wall hangings, safe rattles to shake and manipulate, music, (including singing, humming, etc.) comforting smiles, pats, hugs, and physical warmth.

Space for safe exploration: Allow space for growing body movement: kicking, pushing up on arms to look about, space to roll over, a bassinet or bed that isn't too small. Place objects on a blanket on a floor, and let your baby play on this blanket and try to reach the objects by rolling over.

Encouraging responses: Respond with smiles and verbal encouragement; talk to your child spontaneously while going about normal care. Sing lullabies and recite nursery rhymes.

I can: _____

_____

_____

Six-to-Twelve Months

Sensory stimulation: Provide objects that match growing curiosity and give added sensory experiences such as: plastic blocks to move and stack, plastic mixing spoons and pan, plastic containers of various sizes to stack one inside the other, pans and egg beater, soft toys to cuddle, a lightweight wagon for favorite toys, balls to roll, blocks to build with, and so on. *Read to a child to stimulate a continuing*

feel for the rhythm of words. Give a child books of his own to handle and to help give an appreciation of pictures and the early sight of printed words.

Space for safe exploration: Provide objects on which your child can pull himself or herself up to boost muscle development and develop coordination. Allow space for exploring and discovering. *Provide a safe environment. Remove all dangerous objects from this exploring space.* Foster participation in family activities.

Encouraging response: Be genuine in your delight. Avoid double messages, for instance, a flat statement of "that's good," with a tone of disinterest. Don't respond with voice only. Continue to respond with smiles, pats, touches, and hugs which show the child he or she is valued. Play games such as "Peek-a-Boo," and "Patty-Cake." Talk about all that is experienced through the senses: the soft rug, the smooth cup, the cold water, the warm food, the loud music, the soft voice, and so on. When your child drops early babbling and begins to pattern the sounds heard most often, reinforce these syllables you hear which sound like words familiar to you both, repeating the word correctly:

Child: Da-da . . . da-da . . .

Parent: Here's Daddy. Here's Daddy's boy.

I can: _____

_____

_____

_____

At this six-to-twelve-months age, children continue to tell the differences between various sounds, touches, voices, occurrences in physical surroundings, and the like. They are learning to link actions and results. They cry, and someone comes. They eat, and they feel good. They hurt themselves, and they are comforted. They succeed in continued accomplishments, and you clap your hands and show smiles of approval. They are realizing cause and effect.

FROM TWELVE
TO EIGHTEEN MONTHS

Your children have already entered a period critical to their development. Current research of the Harvard Preschool Project (which has been studying the competency of children since 1965) points to this twelve-eighteen month period as one critical to children's overall competency.

So much is happening during these months; there is an increase of language development and identity, intense curiosity, and the continued push to grow that leads to increased exploration. All of this, these researchers find, can cause parents (or any person who has the main responsibility for caring for the child) a great deal of stress. All of this can force reactions that become patterned in the child. How the mothers (or main caretakers) respond can help form children's identity and their overall idea of people. In fact, so important are these months, that researchers feel much of the basic foundation of education and development will be formed in this twelve-eighteen month period.

Twelve-to-Eighteen-Months

Sensory stimulation: Provide small, easily handled objects to manipulate: measuring spoons, plastic cups, various sizes of balls, unbreakable stacking dishes or objects, plastic containers and lids, shoe boxes and lids, objects to place in these containers, and so on. Provide a variety of playthings that will boost learning through the senses, not only objects to move about, but things to touch, to see, to hear, to smell. Remember that with the intense curiosity to find out about things, your child is likely to taste and handle almost everything in sight. And, continue reading to your child.

Space for safe exploration: Allow space to continue to move about, to walk, to begin to climb. Provide footstools, small chairs, boxes, small toys to ride or pull, containers to help enjoy sand and safe water play.

Encouraging response: As much as possible, continue spontaneous talk related to your child's needs despite the increased demands this age puts upon you. *Use exact language,* the proper names of things (that *box of cereal, not* that *thing).* Respond encouragingly as your child begins to use simple sentences. Add descriptive words to names of objects (a *large green* box), or characteristics to behaviors (running is *fun).* Keep in mind that this is a critical period, that your reactions can have a lifelong impact.

I can: _____

_____

_____

During this time, children literally see things from a different inside and outside view. Inside, they are realizing an increased sense of accomplishment, and your response can help them continue to feel more confident about trying out new things. They need to move to keep discovering. This is a real need, and to deny it can produce frustration.

Words mean much more to them now, and they can well understand more that is said to them than they can say themselves. In addition to their own name and the names of family members, the use of possessive words, "me" and "mine" become increasingly important, for they refer to their growing sense of self as a separate individual.

There is no set number of words children can speak at eighteen months. Some estimates say fifteen—twenty-five words, but I have known a normal child of eighteen months to say only one word. I have also known a child of eighteen months to be able to recite poetry and finish the omitted words of songs sung to him. Do not think you should go about "teaching" your children. Language development comes about during the normal numerous interchanges which give opportunities for spontaneous talk: while dressing and feeding them, taking them on car rides, simply while living.

Whatever your child's rate of development, remember that your child at eighteen months will have concluded one of the most critical of all periods affecting overall competency.

FROM EIGHTEEN MONTHS TO THREE YEARS

Sensory stimulation: Continue to provide many small, easily handled objects including safe kitchen utensils such as spatula and tongs. Continue to provide toys and objects that develop thinking skills and playthings to develop both large and small movement. Help teach responsibility by assigning small tasks: dusting furniture, setting the table, picking up

toys, removing silverware, beginning to put on and take off clothes, and so on. (This also helps develop large and small motor skills and helps your child handle himself or herself in space.) And, of course, continue the "reading pattern."

Space for safe exploration: Provide space for greater freedom to explore and to enjoy the larger play objects. Prevent frustration and allow accomplishment by providing a low stool to stand on for washing hands, brushing teeth, etc., low rods and hooks in the closet for clothes, easily reached shelves for toys and containers for toys. (Colorful plastic tubs can help keep toys in order and are easy to move around).

Encouraging response: Encourage your child to new responsibilities by breaking tasks into several steps. Help master tasks one piece at a time. Talk to your child while showing how to button and unbutton clothing, to zip up zippers, to unbuckle belts, and so on. If you wish, construct a simple cardboard frame and place clothing on it so your child can experiment with small muscle skills. Talk about all of the small movements necessary to manipulate clothing. Help your child learn to recognize and express differences. Talk about the different feel of things: the soft teddy bear, the hard wooden blocks; talk about opposites: small blocks, large blocks; up and down; wet and dry, high and low. Talk about feelings: angry and glad; happy and sad, and so on—and the reasons for the feelings: ("I am sad because I have to work tonight, and I can't be home with you. . . .")

I can: _____

_____

_____

Remember that there is a great increase in language about the age of two—this highlights the overall intense language change during this two-to-three-year period. Three-year-olds are likely to talk to everybody around—family, friends, and themselves. And if you hear your children talking to themselves as they are playing by themselves, know that this gives them a kind of practice at language. It also helps them plan and organize what they are doing as they hear themselves talking it out.

FROM THREE TO SIX YEARS

Sensory stimulation: Provide for painting, coloring, using art materials, safe water and sand play, and working with manipulable games. Provide picture books, large-piece jigsaw puzzles, sorting games of color, shape, and size, safe kitchen utensils, etc.

Space for safe exploration: Allow an opportunity for continuing fine and large motor development: for the use of crayons, pencils, marking pens; for handling adult hammer and nails with supervision; for use of your kitchen "baster" and plastic pail of water (to draw up and let out water); spatula and cardboard for clay pancakes; tongs to lift spoons or other small objects; a medicine dropper and plastic bottles filled with colored water for fine motor development. Provide space for large motor development: running, riding a tricycle and bicycle, building a tree house, and assuming added responsibilities around the home.

Encouraging response: All of this is fertile background for continued talk. Ask and encourage questions. Continue to read to your child and ask questions about what you have read. Continue to help see relationships, to look back, to plan ahead, to see cause and effect, to help identify individual feelings and to relate them to others. Help your child to be honest with feelings by showing that *you* are honest with your feelings. Try to use basically correct vocabulary and sentence structure. Use language that develops thinking skills. All of this provides a base for further exploration when your child leaves the safe environment of home.

I can: _____

_____

_____

SUGGESTIONS FOR DEVELOPING LANGUAGE SKILLS

Throughout the preceding pages, we have used the term "spontaneous talk," as if this kind of talk is natural to all parents. To many parents it is—talking to their children from infancy on, does come easily and naturally. But there are others for whom talking to an

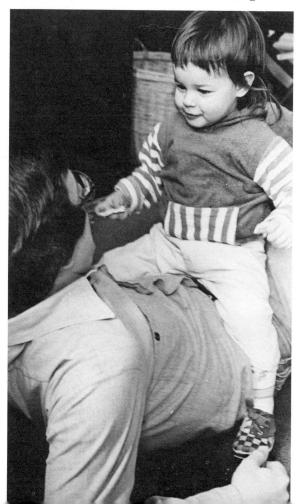

infant or young child is truly difficult. They simply do not know how to go about this.

"Talk to my child? But how do I talk to her?" a young mother of a two-and-a-half year old girl questioned. "I don't know, but the doctor said not to worry, that whenever the speech mechanism was ready, Cindy would talk." Perhaps this parent misunderstood the doctor's advice. At any rate, she did just what she thought the doctor said: she waited until the child's speech mechanism was ready. And she waited, until she heard the simple answer given her by a helpful preschool teacher: "Just talk to her, that's all. There's no real formula for such kind of parent-child talk."

And the mother did start talking to her little girl, but she was very late in doing so. The child, now four, is talking more and more and attending a school in which she receives special help in language skills. Now her mother says, "It is so much easier now that she can talk to me . . . And I'm talking to my younger boy. What you said was really right."

This is not an isolated instance. The mother's experience brings to mind other comments that reflect this very same hesitancy over talking to children: "I feel so sorry for this new baby of a young friend of mine," an acquaintance said recently. "He is just darling, but he is never talked to. His mother tends to him, but she never talks to him. Whenever I get a chance; whenever I'm visiting them, I talk to this baby. It's easy for me."

Another mother responded: "I can relate to that. I was never talked to very much when I was a young child. And I never talked to my baby. I think my daughter will probably be the same—she probably won't talk to her child either."

Their comments reflect the surprise of the mother of a five-year-old girl and a two-year-old boy: "I never knew why singing lullabies—or reading nursery rhymes or poetry—was so important until now. Now I see it gives babies a feeling of language rhythm and an early familiarity with words."

But there is much other talking parents can do, in addition to singing lullabies, that begins to develop language in a very young child. And much of this can be done while going about being parents. The previous pages included suggestions for "spontaneous talk." More specific suggestions are classified according to various stages of growth, but do not think this means that the suggestions fit only the particularly cited stage. Again, it must be stressed: There is no exactly marked-out timetable for language development. That is why one hesitates to classify these examples according to age categories. It is done here only that they can be seen in a relative way. Many of these suggestions can be adopted throughout your child's early years.

And, it bears repeating: these suggestions are just that. Do not think that all of these must be followed. A variety is given so that you can choose only those that appeal particularly to you. *There is no one way for all parents or for all children.*

Developing Language
During Your Child's First Year

The following are suggestions of things you can and should do and things you should not do to help develop language in a young child.

Do's

- From infancy on, recite nursery rhymes, poetry, or sing lullabies to your children. As they grow, they will be aware, not only of the rhythm of the words, but also of the sounds themselves and of the sounds associated with them. In this way, they will become familiar with words, rhythmic patterns of words and sentences, and with word meanings.

- Hold your baby close while you sing lullabies, recite nursery rhymes or poetry. In this way, you will be developing various senses: the sense of touch blends in with the sense of hearing and the sense of sight and the sound of words.

- Use feeding time as a time to talk or sing to your infant children as you hold them close. When they are older, talk to them about the food they are eating: "This is your cereal. Doesn't that taste good?", or "Look, here's your new pink cup for your milk. We'll put this on your tray."

- Avoid saying things as "wa-wa" and "dink" for "water" and "drink." Just use the words correctly as you respond to your child, adding related words of your own: "Here's your drink of water. You like that don't you?" Ask yourself, "If I reinforce a pattern of baby talk from the beginning of this talk time, at what age should I change from baby talk to natural speech patterns?"

- From the time they are very young, use specific words to describe the situation and activity they are involved in. Say things such as, "This is your yellow blanket," or "Here are your carrots," or "See this silver cup Aunt Grace gave you."

- Let your very young children see that you yourself like books and reading material.
- Provide your children with picture books of their own. "Read" the pictures to them.

Don't's

- Continually talk to young children in the same "baby talk" language they use. If they say, "I seepy . . ." for "I am sleepy . . ." for instance, use this type of language in talking to them.
- At feeding time, prop up the bottle with a pillow and go on to other tasks.
- Think that children cannot understand your words anyway, so it's foolish to talk to them while tending to them. At this time, plan other activities and let your mind dwell on far-removed plans.
- Keep your child in a play pen for most of his or her waking hours. Don't allow any space for exploring while your child is so young and curious. Think that at ten months there will be plenty of time for moving about when your child is better coordinated and is better able to understand the meanings of words.

Try to be relaxed in your vocation of parenthood. Children will absorb your relaxed attitude. Do not feel you have to *teach* your child. It is as a father said, "I simply am not going to force Paul to learn. There's so much he can learn from the world; he can learn from all around him."

Language can really develop with living. Just try to give your children a chance to explore and use their developing muscles; remember that learning comes through the senses, and provide them with a variety of sensory stimulations; and remember that children need loving responses through your own talk. Remember also, from infancy on, children respond to the human touch and voice. It begins their humanization. And even when they are very young, an environment with books can instill in children the feeling that books are part of their world. They can absorb this feeling as much as they absorb your use of language.

Developing Language
During Your Child's Second Year

The following suggestions are examples of activities which can promote language in one-to-two-year-old children. Read each and check any you would like to share with your child.

_____ Make a book with pictures your child can feel. Use yarn for hair, cotton for a beard, heavy colorful fabric for clothes, etc. in making "people" pictures. Talk to your child about the different feel of the pictures and the different items of clothing in the book.

_____ Stress names of familiar things: doll, dog, names of family members, and so forth. As you go about your day, talk about things around you—the trees, water, soap, duck, book. Add descriptive words to nouns: the *pretty* trees, the *slippery* soap, the *yellow* duck, the *little* book.

_____ Identify behaviors with people, pets, and playthings: *kiss* momma, *pat* doggie, *wave* by-bye, *love* doll, *rock* dollie.

_____ Even before they might be able to answer you, ask questions. If they are able to answer, value and respect their answers: "Where should we put the toys?" "Should your teddy bear be put on the shelf?" "Would you like to go on the bus to see Aunt Sue?" . . . "You would like to keep your teddy bear on the chair? . . . That's a good idea."

_____ Share opinions and minor problem-solving decisions involving your children. Say things such as, "I think it would be a good idea if we could put these toys on these low shelves. This way we could get them more easily," or "I believe we should sort out some of your toys. Let's put some of these away for now, and then we can get some out at a later time," or "I bought you this little green pail so you could carry your toys in it when we go shopping. Then, you can play with them while I am busy. Do you want to put some toys in the pail now?"

Developing Language
From Eighteen Months to Three Years

This group of suggestions contains activities to share with children as young as eighteen months. You will notice that there is an overlap between this and the preceding period. This is because there is no one time for children to enjoy the suggested activities. Some children younger than eighteen months can also enjoy these. In the same way, children older than three years can find delight in many of these suggestions. And they may also stimulate ideas of your own. As you read the following list, check those you particularly wish to follow. Rank their order of importance to you, from one to five. Use *one* for the suggestions which particularly appeal to you.

_____ Play games of question and answer, each taking a turn at questioning the other.

_____ As you go on walks and trips in the car, find letters of family names on trucks, billboards, storefronts, and so on.

_____ Give your children inexpensive paper and water color crayons or marking pens with which they can express themselves. Be interested in what they make.

_____ Play "pretend" games with them. "Let's pretend you are Daddy and going to work." "Let's pretend you are the television announcer."

_____ Help them see cause and effect. "I have to start supper now, so it will be ready when Daddy comes home." "I have to go to the store to buy the groceries, so we will have them to eat tomorrow."

_____ Talk about relationships to add these concepts to language. "This is a big book. Now, here is a little book." "I'll turn off the light, and then you can go to sleep. Now, it's dark. Tomorrow, it will be light. Then you can get up."

_____ Talk to them about shapes, colors, and so on. "Here's a cookie. See this is a round cookie. The top of this glass is round also. And the top of this pen is round."

These examples are some of the almost limitless ways in which your talk can develop your children's early language and thinking. Whether talking "on the run" or by taking special time, you can use words to describe color, shape, size, opposites, and relationships. In this way your children can begin to absorb these invaluable aids to intellectual development.

Examples of Effective and Non-Effective Dialogue

You have seen how, during these early years, your talk can be extremely helpful in helping your children's talk. And your overall responses can affect your child's entire competency—both positively and negatively. Examples of such effective and noneffective talk are listed below. Read each example, and underline anything that you are not doing now but would like to do. Then, following each of the illustrations, write an example of your own that illustrates effective dialogue.

Parents do not have to feel they always have to stop everything when the child asks for something. Give an honest answer to help your child know what you are feeling. Begin your answers with "I" to help prevent putting unjust blame on the child.

This: I really can't look at your book now. I'm in a real rush. I'll look at it as soon as I can after I make this phone call.

Not this: For crying out loud! Can't you see I'm busy!

This: _____

Build upon the child's words, but don't throw in so much talk that your child tunes you out.

This: *Child* (as he points to mother's skirt): Pants.

Mother: Pants? No, this is Momma's skirt. These are Jimmy's pants. See, Jimmy has red pants. Momma has an orange skirt.

Not This: *Child:* Pants.

Mother: Pants? Don't you know the difference between pants and a skirt? Does this really look like pants? You had better learn the difference or the other kids will make fun of you.

This: _____

This: *Child:* Teddy bo . . . Teddy bo . . .

Mother: (tucking the child in bed): You want your teddy bear? Here's your nice teddy bear. I bet he's tired, too. Love teddy bear. Then, kiss Momma goodnight.

Not this: *Child:* Doggie . . . Doggie!

Parent: Just a minute. You'll get your doggie in a minute. First, I have to change your diaper. Maybe, tonight you'd like your teddy bear instead of your doggie. John gave you the teddy bear, and you don't play with him at all. He's always asking you how you like it. Don't you want the teddy bear? See how soft the teddy bear is. Doggie doesn't feel soft at all. I like soft things. Your blanket is soft. And, I like teddy bear because he is brown and fuzzy . . . .

Bedtime is not the time to stimulate children with too many sensory impressions. Too much language at any time can turn the children off to words.

This: _____

Helpful talk can add related ideas.

This: Get your coat, and we'll go to the store. . . . No, not your blue coat. That is your good coat. You need your green coat—the coat you play in.

Not this: *Mother* (to another mother): If I let my eighteen-month old get his own clothes like you do, I'd be forever waiting for him. Then, it's only more work for me. The other day I let him get his coat, and he pulled down two other jackets. And, you know who had to pick up those!

This: _____

Encouraging responses help teach responsibility.

This: That really is a big help to me when you try to pick up the newspapers. See, you picked up a lot! Now, I don't have to do that, and the house looks much neater.

Not this: You were supposed to pick up all the papers, and you dropped half of them. Can't you see that you can't carry them that way? It's dumb to carry so many at once.

This: _____

Help a child feel good about responsibilities as you show how they can be done, one step at a time.

This: See, you can put the fork on this side of the plate, the left side. Do you want to put all of the forks on the left side of the plate? Tomorrow, you can put the knives on the other side of the plate.

Not this: You can set the table when you are older. Don't bother me about it now.

This: _____

Language and intellectual development are built through interchanges such as this. It is through such interchanges that the entire person is formed.

Developing Language in the Three-to-Six-Year-Old

The patterns we began in early years can continue in these before-school years of three, four, and five. They can continue to build responsibility, identity, creativity, and intellectual development. For these are the years when you can continue to:

- *Help your child see relationships and use imagery:*
  - —"The moon is like a golden ball in the sky."
  - —"Grandmother is your daddy's mother. Great-grandmother is grandmother's mother."
  - —"What do the snowflakes remind you of? I think they are like pieces of cotton stuck to the window."
  - —Give your child several sets of different-sized objects to sort out according to size—from small to large.
- *Help your child plan ahead:*
  - —"Sally goes to kindergarten now. Next year, you will be in kindergarten. Then, first grade."

—"No, let's not wear this shirt today. Tomorrow, you will be going to John's birthday party, and let's save it until then."

- *Help your child identify his feelings:*
  —"I know you're sad because you can't find Ernie. I like Ernie, too. He is really a good puppet."

- *You can state your feelings and why you feel the way you do. This can give your child a pattern for sharing feelings:*
  —"I am angry that you made so much noise while I was on the telephone."

- *Help your child identify feelings by accepting them:*
  —When your child says, "I angry with you," or the equivalent, don't burst into an angry tirade or feel guilty or that you are not a perfect parent. Just respond with a simple statement or question such as, "You're angry with me?" (Be careful of the non verbal communication you reflect). This can be a door opener to let your child really tell you how he or she feels and why.

- *Help your child solve problems:*
  —"I know you don't like Scott to get into your room. He's only two, though, so he isn't really bad when he gets in your things. How do you think we can keep him from getting at your things? . . . You'd like a lock on your door? Well, I think that could be done. I'll go to the hardware store tomorrow and see what kind I can use for your room."

- *Help your child recognize differences between shapes:*
  (As in other learning activities, older children in the family can enjoy this with their younger brother or sister.)
  - —Provide a set of shapes made from light weight cardboard. Print labels on them: square, circle, triangle, rectangle. Have your children place each shape on a similarly shaped object in your home—tables, cabinet doors, plates, etc. Say the names of the shapes and objects aloud: "Yes, the *table* is *rectangle.*" "The *plate* does make a *circle.*"
  - —Draw these shapes on a piece of paper, or have your child trace around these shapes on paper and then color the square, red; the circle, blue; the triangle green; the rectangle, orange. Vary the use of colors as you *continue to talk* about shapes. The cardboard shapes (above) can be matched to these paper shapes.
- *Help your child arrange activities and objects in categories:*
  - —Cut out, or if your child is able to use blunt scissors, have him or her cut out pictures of animals, birds, people, and so on; then arrange these pictures in proper classifications naming the classifications aloud as you go along.
  - —Have an assortment of buttons, coins, paper clips, and so on. Show how these items can be sorted into categories, again talking about what you are doing.
  - —Help your child see the proper order of things. Talk about things you do in the

morning, in the afternoon, in the evening. Ask him or her to tell you a story about getting ready to go to the store, or about anything which shows the order of events, to help your child properly verbalize sequence of activities.

- *Help your child see analogies:*
  —Use family members' names to show analogies: ("I am your father just as Uncle John is Bobby's father.") Have several sizes of circles and triangles. Show the relationship between the larger and smaller size of each. ("This circle is larger than that circle, just as this triangle is larger than that triangle.")

- *Help your child continue to show patterns of correct speech:*
  —*Child:* I go yesterday.
  —*Parent:* You went yesterday? Did you have a good time?

Remember that talking, as exemplified in these activities, will add to vocabulary and also give a base for developing intellectual skills. Of course, preparation for this really begins when your child is an infant. All of the experiences stored in your child's mind from that time on will be there to relate to and add meaning to language and later to printed words—and to reading.

Choose two activities appropriate for your child's stage of development that you would like to try during the coming week. Don't spend too much time worrying whether one activity is "better than" the other. Make your choices and write them below.

Goal: During the next week, I will try to _____

_____

_____

_____

Refer to the remaining activities during the coming weeks. You can continue to choose one or two that appeal to you to share with your child each of the following weeks. In setting goals, be sure they are realistic, attainable goals. Do not go overboard in goal setting. The outcome will be much more positive if you avoid trying too hard, pushing too much, or approaching all of this with an air of "I must do this, or I will be a failure as a parent!"

PLAYING GAMES THAT HELP DEVELOP LANGUAGE

Turn spare, or not-so-spare, moments into game times to boost language learning. As you are doing this, you can help develop the listening, visual, verbal, and comprehension skills needed for later reading. Approach these games with a spirit of delight in words, and your children will catch your spirit. They are likely to absorb, for life, the feeling that using words is fun, that learning can make them feel good about themselves. You can begin each of the following suggestions with words such as, "Let's play a game of. . ." After a time, don't be surprised if your child comes to you and says, "Let's play a game of words."

Many of the following ideas have been used by parents while they were going about daily activities: caring for their children, preparing meals, doing repairs, shopping, traveling, and the like. At times, work can be briefly stopped to focus on a particular activity. But mostly, these can develop spontaneously. Read over these ideas and check those which you would like to share with your child.

To Help Develop a Sense of Rhyme

From infancy on, sing lullabies or recite children's poetry or nursery rhymes to your children. The rhythm of music or poetry combined with words can help them become aware of the rhythmical patterns of language. As they grow, they can be more aware, not only of the rhythm, but of sounds and words and meanings associated with them. Children have fun with rhymes which also help them to discriminate between the different beginning sounds of words that have similar sounding endings.

You can begin by talking about rhymes and how words sound when they rhyme. Give the children various examples of rhymes from the verses with which they are familiar. Then you can use your own made-up verses. Or you can use the following examples and tell your children to add the word that completes the rhyme. (These quick games can be played while you are doing household tasks, but if you wish, you can take the time to print the uncompleted rhymes on separate cards; and, as your children say the word, you can print in their own words. They will enjoy seeing their spoken words take the form of printed words.)

- I go to the store and I look and I look
  on every shelf for a story ___(book)___.
- In the night
  We turn off the ___(light)___.
- I like to stop
  At the ice-cream ___(shop)___.
- Up in the sky, so very far
  I see a tiny, shining ___(star)___.

To Help Recognize Sounds and Letters

- Play a simple naming game along the lines of the following.
- *Parent:* This is the way we can play "I'm going to the store." I'll start by saying, "I'm going to the store to buy something that begins with *B*." Remember *B* sounds like *Buh* in the word *baby*. Say *baby*. Hear the *buh* sound. There is also a *buh* sound in bear and in boxes and in ball. All right, let's begin. I'm going to the store to buy something that begins with *B*. I'm going to buy *beans*. Now, it's your turn. You say what you're going to buy that begins with

B. Begin by saying, "I'm going to the store to buy something that begins with *B*." Then tell me something you buy which begins with the sound of *B*.

- Buy a box of magnetic letters to place on the refrigerator or metal surface. Play a "Find-the-letter" game. Say a word to your child. Tell him the first sound that is heard in the word and the letter the word begins with. Then have your child find the letter. Proceed from letter to letter, beginning with the consonants (all the letters except the vowels, a, e, i, o, and u).

- Name a letter with which your child is familiar, or use the sound of the letter. Have your child name as many words as possible which begin with the sound or with the letter you name.

- Help your child make an alphabet book. Use 27 sheets of heavyweight paper. (Heavy grocery sacks will work well.) Punch holes in each page and lace the pages together with cord. Print a letter of the alphabet on every other page with a large marking pen. Opposite each letter page, paste a large manilla envelope (or an envelope of your own which you made). Have your child cut pictures of objects and name the object and the sound of the beginning letter, then put the objects into the appropriate envelopes.

To Help Teach Colors, Shapes, and Lines

- Use a box of colored toothpicks. First have your child match colors. Then make slanting, perpendicular, and horizontal lines and squares, triangles, and rectangles with the toothpicks, and have your child match those.

- Young children are often fascinated with the letter with which their own names begin. A child, whose name begins with *T*, for instance, can find all of the *T's* on the street signs, on boxes of cereal and groceries in the store, in magazines, and so on.

To Help Appreciate
Sounds of New Words

- Play a game of naming new words: Say "I'm going to give you a special word today. I like this word. Your new word is *delicious. De-lic-ious. Delicious.* Now, can you say delicious? See, how that word rolls around in your mouth?"
Choose words that have a melodious tone. Do not necessarily choose simple words, for your child will enjoy not only the sounds and the way the word feels on the tongue, but mastery of a word more complicated than anything ever said before. Words such as beautiful, precious, glamorous, and the like can be used. It is not necessary that your child even know the meaning for the word, at this time, but later use these words naturally in your vocabulary, in order that their meanings can be absorbed.
- Try a combination of unusual sounding words such as "chick-a-dee, bumble bee, nanny goat, and bananas." A child can delight in these sounds.

To Help Them Try Out
Different Roles and Language
Associated with These Roles

Play "Let's Pretend" games. Encourage your child to act out characters in fairy tales, nursery rhymes, television programs, or even interchange your own parent-child roles.

Developing Meanings
and Habits with Words

Language is not just using words and symbols attached to objects; it is also the whole range of internal meanings we hold for words. These meanings for words are influenced by our background and how we first heard the words used. How children hear words used not only contributes to their meanings for words but to their impression of themselves as well.

Consider the following expressions which can convey negative impressions especially if accompanied by negative, non-verbal cues (frowns, loud voices, tones of anger, shame, or ridicule, or the like). After each statement, convey the same message, but use different words to give the child a positive image of himself or herself.

   1. What a pack rat you are!

   Your statement: ――――――――――

   ――――――――――――――――――――

   2. Clean up your junk!

   Your statement: ――――――――――

   ――――――――――――――――――――

3. What a filthy mess your room is—Ugh!

Your statement: _____

_____

4. You're such a nuisance, climbing up on my lap as soon as I want to read the paper.

Your statement: _____

_____

5. Cut out that racket!

Your statement: _____

_____

6. You want a doll? Little boys don't play with dolls. Sissy!

Your statement: _____

_____

7. You wet the bed? Aren't you ashamed of yourself? Kindergarten children don't wet the bed. Baby!

Your statement: _____

_____

8. Get out of that toilet! You're a bad, bad girl!

Your statement: _____

_____

9. Crying! Boys don't cry. Only girls cry.

Your statement: _____

_____

You might think it makes no difference whether you say, "Clean up your junk—I can't stand the sight of it anymore. You're so messy." or "In fifteen minutes it will be bedtime, and you should have all your scraps of paper and crayons picked up by that time." But the two statements are very different to a child.

Of course, the nonverbal communication that accompanies such statements can completely change the message. Examples 1, 2, and 5 for instance, are not necessarily harmful if they would be accompanied with a smile or a nondisapproving tone of voice.

But comments such as these, if they are consistent, can influence adult responses. And constant arguments, threats, or yelling, can have especially long-lasting effects as a worn-out young mother explained:

> I always resolved I would never raise
> my child the way I was treated, and
> now I find I'm doing the same thing.
> My boy is five. I get terribly angry
> with him, and end up smacking him.
> I don't want to raise my kids the way
> I've been raised—and here I find
> myself doing the same thing. He's
> already raising his fist to me. He's seen
> his father and I go at each other
> from the time he was born, so he's
> really doing just what we have been
> doing. He's really imitating us.

This mother really did not want to treat her boy the same way as she had been treated, and yet she found herself doing the same thing and acting the same way. It is a powerful testimony to the effect that parents' actions and language have on their children—and their children's children. You should remember this when you think your patterns of communication do not matter.

Helping Your Child
Become Aware of Printed Words

The previous activities focused on helping your children become aware of spoken words. But there are a variety of other things one can do which can help children find enjoyment in written words. Like the previous suggestions, they take very little time. Read each of the suggestions below and rank them in the order ("1" for most on down to "5" for least) of their appeal to you. Underline the activity or activities you rated "1" and resolve to follow one suggestion at least once during the next week.

_____ Call attention to words seen around them: Stop, go, slow, etc.

_____ Make labels of items of their clothes and have them place the label on the corresponding item of clothing. (You can print the names of clothing on note cards or paper). Have them say the first letter of the label and tell you its sound. Then, if possible, have them tell you another word which begins with the same sound as the word on each label. ("Dress"—begins with _d_. Another word that starts with _d_ is "dog.")

_____ Cut out (or have your children cut out with blunt scissors) pictures of things with which they are familiar. They can cut out favorite foods, clothes, objects, places, and so on. Identify a set of small boxes with several letters of the alphabet. (These letters can be changed according to the letters your children continue to learn.) Children can sort these cut outs into the appropriately lettered box. The boxes could also be identified with words such as foods, clothes, toys, etc., and your children can sort the pictures into these separate classifications.

_____ Names of family members and friends are interesting to children. Mark off a sheet of heavy cardboard in nine squares. In each square, print the name of a family member or friend. Give your children a corresponding set of squares on which the same names are printed. Have them place each name on the matching name in the squares. As they are familiar with the names, vary this activity by calling out names on the card and have your children match appropriate cards with the names on the larger card.

_____ Help your children make their own picture books by pasting pictures from magazines on inexpensive paper. (Staple or lace the pages together.) One picture should be pasted on every other page. Tell them that they can "read" to you what the pictures are about, and you can write in the words they have used. This way they can "write" their own original books.

At the beginning of these suggestions, you were asked to rank these examples (1-5) in the order of their appeal to you and underline the most popular activities. Now, choose one of these underlined suggestions, and write this in the form of a goal: During the next week, I will try to _____

_____

_____

Goals should be stars to focus upon. It is not that you can reach them completely, but you can try to come closer to their brightness. You can keep working toward weekly goals. You can continue your goal setting as the weeks unfold.

HELPING LANGUAGE COME TO LIFE

Your talk can form your child's view of the world. You can help make it colorful and exciting or dull and lifeless depending how you use words. Simple ways to make our language come to life are described below.

Using Specific Language

Begin using specific words during your child's very first year. Continue doing so to improve communication. Example A, which follows, uses specific language. Example B uses nonspecific language. Read each example and circle each nonspecific word in example B. On a separate sheet of paper write a specific word or words for the ones you circled and read the statements over, using the specific terms. Do you see how much clearer it is and how the use of specific language helps your child to understand the uses of words?

A: Let's make a poster of yourself as a surprise for your dad when he comes home tomorrow. First, I'll get the roll of wallpaper that we're not going to use anymore. All we need is the roll of wallpaper, a scisssors, and a pencil and marking pen to get started.

Here is the wallpaper, scissors, pen, and pencil. Now, I'll tear off a piece of paper larger than you are. See, that's about one foot taller than you.

Now, I'll put the paper on the floor, and you lie down on the paper while I trace around you with the pencil. . . . There, I'm finished, and you can get up. See this line makes an outline of you. That's you.

Now, that we have that much finished, let's make this poster really be you. To do that, we'll use this marking pen and write your name on the poster. Now, tell me words that describe you and we'll write them down on the poster.

B: "Let's make something for Dad for when he comes home tomorrow. Lie down on this paper, and I'll trace around you. Then, we can cut it out and fill it with things. Tell me some words, and I'll put them in."

Sometimes, we can fall into the habit of continually using unclear and vague statements such as the following. Change these general statements to lively and specific language as indicated in the first example.

1. This tastes O.K.
   <u>This ice cream is delicious!</u>

2. They played a bit.

_____

3. I'll be there soon.

_____

4. Bring me that, and we'll fix this.

_____

5. Put that there.

_____

6. Those are all over.

_____

We all use language such as this from time to time. The thing to remember is—don't do it all the time; don't give your child a pattern of "lazy" language. Of course, there are no right or wrong answers to the above. Sample statements could be something like these: "John and Joe played for at least two hours." "I'll be with you in about five minutes." "Could you put the book on the table, please?" "The buttons are all over the floor." Children are great imitators. Help them imitate lively language.

TELEVISION, LANGUAGE, AND THOUGHT

Television is a powerful medium, and has caught both praise and criticism for its effect upon children. In any case, it is part of our lives, and you can try any of these suggestions of ways to use television to add to language and learning. Check those you wish to try. Add ideas of your own.

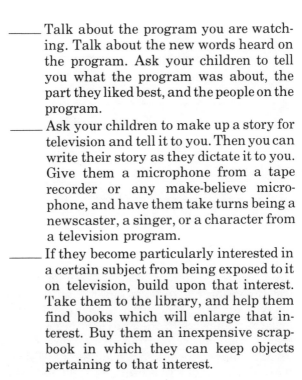

_____ Talk about the program you are watching. Talk about the new words heard on the program. Ask your children to tell you what the program was about, the part they liked best, and the people on the program.

_____ Ask your children to make up a story for television and tell it to you. Then you can write their story as they dictate it to you. Give them a microphone from a tape recorder or any make-believe microphone, and have them take turns being a newscaster, a singer, or a character from a television program.

_____ If they become particularly interested in a certain subject from being exposed to it on television, build upon that interest. Take them to the library, and help them find books which will enlarge that interest. Buy them an inexpensive scrapbook in which they can keep objects pertaining to that interest.

I can: _____

_____

This is not to say that indiscriminate television viewing is helpful to children. Television programs should be chosen with an eye to their content. As with the books you choose to read to your children, this can enrich their lives, not just entertain or add to a skill in using words.

A LOOK BACK

At the beginning of this section, you were asked to complete a self-inventory. Now, go back to this inventory to reassess yourself. What different insights do you now have about your part in developing language competency in your children? In what ways have you changed?

I feel _____

_____

_____

Go back to the very first inventory. In what ways have you changed since that time?

_____

_____

You have felt the growth that comes along with change. As you continue to change, remember it is not that change always makes life easier, but that it can make life more valuable. If particular changes or realizations make more demands upon you, accept the challenge. Meet it with courage. Then, you will not only feel that you are developing inner resources in your children—but that you are developing inner resources in yourself.

Because this section includes a variety of suggestions for helping children use language, remember that underlying all of them is one key: a loving response to the *individual* child's needs. It must be remembered that children are very individual: quiet, outgoing, spontaneous, thoughtful. Some are naturally more talkative than others. A loving response means keeping your individual child in mind.

Remember that language is a creative experience. Remember that becoming oneself is a

creative experience, and that the two should go hand in hand. Remember what was said in the preceding section on creativity: Stimulate. Don't stifle. Don't think that all the suggestions must be followed. Helpful as they are, they are not "exercises to be dutifully undertaken." As pointed out in earlier sections of this book, a balance must be kept in mind. Remember that sometimes the best response we can give our child is our silence.

For children need mental space to be creative in developing their own language, to think about what you have read or said to them, to try out adult roles in play, to sort out their feelings, to talk out their problems, and to make sense of it all. Overhearing two-to-three-year-old children's solitary conversations shows us this: ("Here I been tryin' to be good. I didn't interrupt or anything." "Here is your little girl lying in bed, crying her heart out." "I put man in car." "Daddy flyin' to Chicago.")

Children need mental space to let life sink into them, and to plan out how they fit into life. Providing them mental space is part of our overall encouraging, loving responses.

In all of the suggestions we saw how such encouraging responses are vital in fostering curiosity and further motivation for learning. Such an environment allows the child to feel free to roam, inspect, and learn. It provides for stimulating growth. In this environment, the parents are available to the child—even if they are not at home all of the time. In this environment, learning is developed. This underscores what many parents themselves say:

A father: My wife and I talked to both of our children as we would talk to each other. We used language in adult sentences—just as if they could understand. I think talking to kids is part of an attitude. It is only beneficial if you have something to say to them, not just talking to be saying words in a rote like, teaching fashion.

A mother of a four-year-old: When my children were very young, I read a lot to them, played all kinds of word games with them. I did this because I had trouble learning to read, and I didn't want my children to have the same kind of trouble I had.

A mother of a four-year-old, a two-year-old, and a one-year-old child: Yes, Molly can read. But, we never really taught her. We have always taken her to the library with us, and from the time she was about fifteen months old, she began fooling around with books. She actually began reading when she was about three and a half. I really think television has helped with her letters and sounds. *Sesame Street* and *The Electric Company* completely absorbed her. She apparently had the attention span for that, but my next child is different. He has a different attention span.

Molly's grandmother: I talked a lot to my children. I just didn't understand baby talk. I also sang a lot to them—when I was hauling the older kids back and forth to school. Now my daughters both sing a lot to their own children.

And **a mother employed away from home:** As often as possible in the time we have together, I play games such as "Opposites" with Jerry. We each say the opposite of the word the other has said: hot/cold; up/down; on/off, and so on. His dad and I play a word game with him that helps him become familiar with saying compound words: postman/post office; bookmark/bookcase and the like. Of course, we don't do this all the time. I always believed in giving Jerry time by himself. I started way before he was a year old. I'd play with him for awhile, and then I would let him play by himself for at least twenty minutes. It was something I remember my mother doing with us when we were children . . . . Now, he's three, and sometimes he says, "Well, Mom, I just thinkin' now. I just thinkin'. I thinkin' about trucks." He's using language in his mind.

This child shows us that using language does not necessarily mean using spoken language. He is using language in his mind as he is learning to find his place in life.

These parents' statements demonstrate the effectiveness of positive interaction in developing language. These parents have shown their children a lively enthusiasm and respect for language and for the children's individuality. They have experienced the adventure of helping bring their children to language and to living and to all that language and living mean. They have helped their children cross the bridge that spans human aloneness.

Their kind of response gives children more than words. It tells them that someone listens, pays attention, respects, and values them. This kind of response tells them they belong. This can help give them freedom to find continuing newness about them. It can help children feel free enough to examine this newness—to feel free to draw upon their own thoughts and to share them with others.

And, as you help your children find this newness, they reflect back to us their fresh insights, their sense of wonder, their uncluttered vision. It is a two-way street. Sharing together helps both children—and parents—continue to grow.

CONCLUSION

Your responses to your children help develop language—and much more: They affect each child's physical, emotional, social, and intellectual makeup. They do not form the *entire* child, for each child is an individual with his or her own makeup, but they do much to develop a child's overall personality and competency.

A parent's responses include more than just talking to a child. They include the entire "answer" given to each child's needs. And so the responses to a child's need for security, responsibility, achievements, and limits; to the need for freedom and space to explore; the responses to the need for love and the need to realize one is loveable and worthwhile all help to give a child a lifelong base for security and identity and the feeling that the world itself is a place to trust.

Your responses help develop an inner sense of self-esteem and worth which can enhance a child's entire life. Your responses help develop independence and a spirit of enterprise, to create, to experiment, and to change. And, of course, your responses can help a child express what he or she is experiencing.

With these inner resources children learn to trust themselves—and not to be afraid of failure. They learn not to be afraid of reaching out to others. Your responses can help them continue one of the most creative tasks they have to face—to keep becoming themselves.

At the outset of this book the need for *very early* responses to your child was stressed, for the ages before three are critical to a child's competency. This does not take away the need for continuing responses in the after-three-year-old period.

Children never outgrow their need for love and affirmation. Now, in these infancy-to-six years, with their absorbing psyche, they draw into themselves the kind of persons they are and what they can do—from continuing impressions drawn from the people and the environment closest to them. In the years after six, however, impressions from others will increasingly join with impressions received from you as parents to add to each child's "inner-picture." The responses that are important now, they will continue to be important.

A teacher of three-to nine-year-old children put this very clearly:

It's amazing, I could go right down the list of my children and tell you whose parents value their work—who appreciate it. It reflects in the child, and not only in his skill development. It is just that the parents' responses help the children love learning. And then you can teach them.

I always give my children a choice of taking their work home or hanging it on the wall at school, and some children choose to hang their work right here in school, knowing that here it will receive recognition, but that it won't get any recognition at home.

From about the time children are in

225

kindergarten or six years old, parents give over too much responsibility to the school. We at school, however, cannot give children the kind of response that parents give. School is exciting for children because it means something to parents.

To you, who are parents of six-year-old children "moving on," her statements are a special challenge for the years ahead—to continue to give them the kind of responses that will help—for life.

You have already done much. From their outer environment, you have helped form the nucleus of inner resources. These inner resources will be the basis of the later strengths they will need: the strength of having their own convictions, to test their own values against those of others; the strength to cope, to meet change, the strength to form inner controls, to resist powerful tides that can press against them in a fast-moving world; the strength to hope in themselves and also to be able to draw sustenance from others, to know and respect their own individuality, and to know what they can contribute to the human family.

Your children have already gone such a long way. They still have a long way to go . . . . What kind of response will you make in their journey?

BIBLIOGRAPHY
REFERENCES

Abraham, Willard. *Living with Preschoolers.* Phoenix, Arizona: O'Sullivan, Woodside & Company. 1976.

Beadle, Muriel. *A Child's Mind.* New York: Doubleday, 1971.

Beck, Joan. *How to Raise a Brighter Child.* New York: Simon and Schuster, Pocket Books, 1975.

Bettleheim, Bruno. *The Uses of Enchantment: The Meaning and Importance of Fairy Tales.* New York: Random House, 1977.

Briggs, Dorothy Corkille. *Your Child's Self-Esteem: The Key to His Life.* Garden City, New York: Doubleday, 1975.

Britton, James. *Language and Learning.* Coral Gables, Florida: University of Miami Press, 1971.

Church, Joseph. *Understanding Your Child from Birth to Three.* New York: Simon and Schuster, Pocket Books, 1977.

Cohen, Martin. "A Warning to Conscientious Mothers." *Readings in Educational Psychology: Contemporary Perspective.* 1976-1977 edition, Harper and Row, 1976.

Dentler, Robert A. and Bernard Shapiro, eds. *Readings in Educational Psychology: Contemporary Perspectives.* 1976-1977 edition, Harper and Row, 1976.

Dreikurs, Rudolf. *The Challenge of Child Training.* New York: Hawthorn Books, 1972.

Dreikurs, Rudolf, and Loren Grey. *Logical Consequences: A New Approach to Discipline.* New York: Hawthron Books, 1968.

Fraiberg, Selma H. *The Magic Years.* New York: Charles Scribner, 1968.

Hayakawa, Samuel I. *Symbol, Status, and Personality.* Harcourt Brace Jovanovich, 1966.

Hurlock, Elizabeth B. *Child Development.* New York: McGraw Hill, 1973.

Larrick, Nancy. *A Parent's Guide to Children's Reading,* Fourth Edition. New York: Bantam Books, 1975.

Miller, Maureen. *Family Learning Center Workshops—A Series for Growth and Getting Along Together.* Des Moines, Iowa: Project prepared under Grant from U.S. Office of Education, HEW, 1975.

Moustakas, Clark ed. *The Child's Discovery of Himself.* New York: Ballantine Books, 1975.

Overstreet, Bonaro W. *Understanding Fear in Ourselves and Others.* New York: Harper and Row, 1971.

Pines, Maya. "A Child's Mind is Shaped Before Age Two," *Readings in Educational Psychology: Contemporary Perspectives.* 1976-1977 edition, Robert A. Dentler and Bernard Shapiro, eds. New York: Harper and Row, 1976.

Rogers, Carl. *On Becoming a Person.* Boston, Mass.: Houghton Mifflin, 1961.

Shostrom, Everett. *Freedom to Be.* Englewood Cliffs, New Jersey: Prentice-Hall, 1972.

Strom, Robert, *"Play and Family Development." Readings in Educational Psychology: Contemporary Perspectives.* 1976-1977 edition. Robert A. Dentler and Bernard Shapiro, eds. New York: Harper and Row, 1976.

White, Burton L., et. al. *Experience and Environment.* Englewood Cliffs, New Jersey: Prentice Hall, 1973.

White, Burton L. *The First Three Years of Life.* Englewood Cliffs, New Jersey: Prentice-Hall, 1975.

Your Child from One to Twelve. (Foreword Lee Salk, Ph.D.) New York: New American Library, 1970.